"Inspired by, and supported with, a foreword by David Kinnaman, author of the bestselling *unChristian*, this [book] puts faces on Kinnaman's findings on Christianity's image problem. In four cities, the authors interviewed Christians but also agnostics, atheists, Muslims, gays, and other groups Christians are believed to reject. . . . The combined impact of the book and [videos] is stunning: the authors have heard and noted important ways Christians can improve their outreach by being more like Jesus, who meets people where they are."

—*Publishers Weekly*

"*The Outsider Interviews* is a brilliant reminder to Christians and non-Christians alike that God's love is bigger than our mistakes and that Jesus will continue to survive the embarrassing things we do in his name."

—Shane Claiborne, author and activist, TheSimpleWay.org

"An honest dialogue between those who state that they belong to Jesus and those ranging from 'on the way' to 'no way.' I encourage us all to watch, read, and join the conversation."

—Elisa Morgan, publisher of www.FullFill.org; president emerita of MOPS International; author of *She Did What She Could*

"If you care about the people Jesus cares about, please listen to the voices and messages within."

—Dan Kimball, author of *They Like Jesus but Not the Church*

THE
OUTSIDER
INTERVIEWS

What Young People Think about Faith and How to Connect with Them

Jim Henderson, Todd Hunter, and Craig Spinks

BakerBooks

a division of Baker Publishing Group
Grand Rapids, Michigan

© 2010, 2012 by Jim Henderson, Todd Hunter, and Craig Spinks

Published by Baker Books
a division of Baker Publishing Group
P.O. Box 6287, Grand Rapids, MI 49516-6287
www.bakerbooks.com

Revised and updated edition published in 2012

Printed in the United States of America

Library of Congress Cataloging-in-Publication Data
Henderson, Jim, 1947–
    The ousider interviews : what young people think about faith and how to connect with them / Jim Henderson, Todd Hunter, and Craig Spinks. — Rev. and updated ed.
        p.   cm.
    Includes bibliographical references.
    ISBN 978-0-8010-1424-6 (pbk.)
    1. Christianity. 2. Interviews. 3. Generation Y—Religious life. 4. Postmodernism—Religious aspects—Christianity. I. Hunter, Todd D., 1956– II. Spinks, Craig. III. Title.
BR124.H45 2012
270.084'2—dc23   2012023721

Unless otherwise indicated, Scripture quotations are from *The Message* by Eugene H. Peterson, copyright © 1993, 1994, 1995, 2000, 2001, 2002. Used by permission of NavPress Publishing Group. All rights reserved.

Scripture quotations labeled KJV are from the King James Version of the Bible.

Scripture quotations labeled NIV are from the Holy Bible, New International Version®. NIV®. Copyright © 1973, 1978, 1984, 2011 by Biblica, Inc.™ Used by permission of Zondervan. All rights reserved worldwide. www.zondervan.com

Photos of Jim Henderson and Craig Spinks appear courtesy of www.michaelwilsonphotographer.com.

Photos of Todd Hunter appear courtesy of www.tiffanyhixphotography.com.

The internet addresses, email addresses, and phone numbers in this book are accurate at the time of publication. They are provided as a resource. Baker Publishing Group does not endorse them or vouch for their content or permanence.

12   13   14   15   16   17   18   7   6   5   4   3   2   1

green press INITIATIVE

For *the people Jesus misses most*

CONTENTS

Contents

HALF YOUR BOOK
IS MISSING!

Shortly after opening this book, you'll start to feel as though you're missing something.

That's because you are! This book wouldn't be complete without watching the video footage that the book was based on. The videos capture details and nuances the text can't, so we didn't even try! You can watch the videos all at once or individually alongside their corresponding chapters, but keep in mind that we wrote this book with the assumption that you've watched or will be watching the videos.

To access all of the videos for free, go to OutsiderInterviews.com.

FOREWORD

I am excited about *The Outsider Interviews*.

As a survey researcher and a generational analyst, I am often asked where we actually find the people we interview. Our firm, the Barna Group, conducts telephone, online, and in-person interviews with tens of thousands of people every year. We employ sophisticated survey techniques and high-quality, nationwide samples. But if people read the data from our research and it does not fit their experiences, it is easy for them to wonder about the so-called science of survey research.

This happened frequently as a result of *unChristian*, the book Gabe Lyons and I collaborated on, which describes the next generation's growing disenchantment with Christianity. When the book was released, a lot of people had a hard time imagining that real people embraced such hostile—yet often very nuanced—views about the Christian faith. *Where did you find these people to interview? Why don't I know anyone like this? Do young people really perceive Christianity in such negative ways? None of the young people I know actually understand that much about the Christian faith. Don't young people just think whatever the media tells them to think?*

I am enthusiastic about this book and the video footage that can be found online because I think this project begins to answer questions like these.

Actually, I understand why people are skeptical about research. There is no shortage of data available these days; most of it is not particularly good or reliable. And it is not easy to hear people critiquing the faith many of us follow.

Yet I think this resource from my friends Jim Henderson, Todd Hunter, and Craig Spinks is a fantastic way to get a "street-level" view of what young people think about the Christian faith. I have personally put in loads of hours trying to understand what Christianity looks like from an outsider's perspective, but this tool helped me remember the very human side of the thousands of interviews we have done. The video interviews put flesh and bones to the data—they make the stories come to life *because they involve real lives*.

Beyond the video segments with young people, I think you will be challenged by the insight Jim, Todd, and Craig offer in the book. I participated in many of the live events during which the Outsider Interviews were filmed. I had a close-up look as Jim, Todd, and Craig worked their way from Phoenix to Seattle, Denver to Kansas City, trying to make sense of what they were learning. This book offers their observations filtered with a passion to help people see the real Jesus. I believe many of their observations and insights will stretch you as they did me.

Before letting you loose into reading the book, let me offer one last observation: Isn't it ironic that one of the things that makes us human—our ability to hear and understand subtle inflections of complex sounds known as language—is also something we struggle with the most? Translation: for all our communication abilities, we don't listen very well. I suppose that makes some sense because our ability to communicate is deeply affected by our fallen nature. Just think about the common listening gaps: men versus women; wives against husbands; parents face off with children; employers agitate workers and vice versa; immigrants versus citizens; Christians against non-Christians. No matter what side of the fence you're on, we all struggle to understand others.

That was part of the reason I decided to use the terms "insiders" and "outsiders" in the book *unChristian*: they actually fit the way most of us think. For the most part, we really do consider people "in" or "out," us versus them, Christians and everyone else. Don't get me wrong—I am more convinced than ever that we need to help people understand why they need Jesus. But this takes harder work than ever and better, deeper reservoirs for hearing and perceiving the perspectives of those around us.

Ultimately this resource, like good research itself, should help us become better listeners. It will certainly make it harder to put people into neat little boxes.

Listen in on *The Outsider Interviews* with Jim, Todd, and Craig—three people I admire for their courage and transparency. They have let us in on their conversations and interactions with the next generation in hopes that all of us will grow into better people—more human, better listeners.

I am grateful to these three observers. And I hope they can help me find our next set of survey respondents!

David Kinnaman
Coauthor, *unChristian*
President, Barna Group

ACKNOWLEDGMENTS

Our editor, Chad Allen, is the person most responsible for this book seeing the light of day. He pursued us, put up with us, and pummeled us with questions that kept making the book better and better. He deserves a great deal of the credit for this unique product.

We are also grateful to the people who agreed to participate in this project. The outsiders and insiders who opened their hearts to us fearlessly voiced their opinions and helped us become more authentic followers of Jesus.

Special thanks go to Kathy Escobar, Karl Wheeler, Beth Fitch, and Kirk Wulff. They are the people who spent some of their hard-earned relational capital on this project by recruiting their outsider friends to participate in these interviews. Thanks also go to Mountain View Lutheran Church in Phoenix; Christ Church Anglican in Overland Park, Kansas; Calvary Assembly in Seattle; The Refuge in Denver; and Alpha for providing venues and generous partnership.

It takes a village to write a book. Each one of our families has absorbed our attitudes, late night talks, and strange ideas. Consequently, special thanks go to Todd's wife, Debbie, and his children, Jonathon and Carol Hunter; Craig's wife, Sara, and his dad, Bob Spinks; and Jim's wife, Barbara, his three children, Joshua, Sarah, and Judah, and his first grandson, Huxley (aka "The Huckster") George Henderson.

Finally, it is with gratitude and humility that we acknowledge that *The Outsider Interviews* would have never transpired without the research and inspiration of David Kinnaman and Gabe Lyons's seminal work *unChristian*.

1

THE BACKSTORY

The Why, Where, Who, and How

Craig Spinks

The book *unChristian* quantified something that Jim, Todd, and I had instinctively felt for a long time: a divide between Christians and "outsiders," as well as an internal divide among Christian "insiders."[1] What bothered us more than the divide itself was how entrenched the various sides appear to be in their views. With entrenchment comes name-calling and demonization. Christians become known as hatemongers; everyone else is a hedonistic rebel. Personally, I've found it challenging to not use stereotypes and assumptions as shortcuts in relationships. Listening and trying to understand someone's perspective is time consuming and often challenging. Perhaps you can relate. Maybe you have a son, daughter, parent, grandparent, or friend you find difficult to relate to. Perhaps they are gay, pro-life, liberal, fundamentalist, or part of the tea party movement. Maybe some topics are off-limits or only discussed behind each other's backs. Often we'd like the other person to change, but it's not very often that positive change results from such deep polarization. Trying to better understand another's perspective doesn't come naturally for a lot of us, but the three of us believe that it's one of the best skills we can employ as we encounter difficult situations. Agreement may never come, but we can find ways to navigate difference. This book aims to build bridges, not eliminate divides.

Capturing Stories behind the Statistics

While I love the bird's-eye perspective that statistics offer, they also reduce nuance and complexity down to mere numbers. Behind every stat in *unChristian* there are hundreds of stories. The three of us wanted to tell some of the stories behind these stats, to capture some of the hearts behind the charts. We don't present these stories as an attempt to shift your views or beliefs but rather to help you better listen to those views, especially the ones you disagree with. Perhaps it will even help in your own challenging relationships.

As you begin *The Outsider Interviews*, it might be helpful to understand the methods we used in our interview and writing process. We traveled to four cities and interviewed sixteen young adults between the ages of sixteen and twenty-nine. Some identify themselves as Christian; others don't. Each person was interviewed twice: once as part of a group in front of a room of Christians attending an evangelism conference, then in a more private setting backstage. We referenced the video footage from these interviews as we wrote the book. The book and video footage (which can be seen at OutsiderInterviews.com) work together and are not mutually exclusive. To get the complete picture, read the book and watch the videos.

This project started with Jim Henderson. Jim is an entrepreneur in so many ways, but most notably in his work helping Christians to see themselves through the eyes of outsiders. He started conducting Outsider Interviews even before they were called Outsider Interviews. Todd Hunter and I have known and worked with Jim for over a decade and were obvious choices when Jim had the idea to include several perspectives in the book. Todd has the most theological training of the three of us. His extensive and diverse experience as a leader and pastor give him a unique perspective that grounds our content. On the other hand, I come with more practical experience. When we first started working on this project, I was twenty-eight, which made me part of the demographics Kinnaman and Lyons used in their research. I also brought my experience as a video producer to the project, allowing us to deeply integrate the written content with the video content. But my most meaningful contribution didn't become apparent until after we started writing. The writing process challenged me to work on some of my own difficult relationships, which has helped us capture some of the complexities of dialogue at the street level. But let's not get ahead of ourselves—more on that later.

An Opportunity to Practice

If we did our job correctly, at some point in this book you'll read something that will agitate or upset you. Your mouth will drop open, and you may find yourself yelling at an inanimate object called a book. Ask yourself *why* before rushing through those sections. Try to put yourself in the shoes of the person speaking. Resist the urge to think of counterarguments, and simply focus on the person and their story. Consider why you responded so strongly; what about their story triggered you inside? When we're provoked in real life, our reactions are often clouded by emotion, personal history with the other person, and past experience. There's also often relational equity on the line. As you read this book and watch the interviews, think of it as an opportunity to practice empathy without risk. Notice the moments that agitate you, and lean into those moments. On that note, let's get to it!

2

KANSAS CITY OUTSIDERS

Christianity Has an Image Problem

Jim Henderson

This chapter is based on our Kansas City interview. To get the complete story, be sure to watch the videos online (for free!) at OutsiderInterviews.com/KansasCity.

> I've never had anybody say they want to save me and felt like they truly loved me.
>
> Klarisa

Whenever you and I get serious about change, psychotherapists, personal trainers, football coaches, piano teachers, and premarital counselors become our new best friends. They measure, probe, inspire, and even insult us. And we pay them to do it! A great example of this is the Body-for-LIFE weight loss program. Before you can begin, they require that you submit a "before" photo of you in your swimsuit for all to see. They know that seeing what you really look like in the mirror is the first step to real change.

But programs like Body-for-LIFE provide something else that's needed for real change to happen: a plan, a mental map that can lead us out of the past and into the future. Sometimes this map comes in the form of a person; sometimes it's a story; and sometimes it's three, seven, or twelve steps. Often, it's a combination of all three.

Our Outsider Interviews provide both experiences. On one hand, they're a mirror for Christians to see their reflection through the eyes of outsiders. On the other, they're a map to help insiders understand how to connect with outsiders.

In these interviews we're hoping to inspire Christians to pursue new relationships with outsiders. We want to provide Christians with what we think of as an updated map of the cultural terrain as described by the people who are native to the area. For our purposes, those natives are often young people. Here's why.

If you've had the privilege of living in proximity to an immigrant community, you've likely noticed that the children often translate for the parents. That's because, as psychologist Ken Robinson once said at a conference I attended, "In immigrant communities *the children . . . teach their parents the culture*, the language, and the ideas." We think the same is true for Christians. When it comes to understanding the socio-spiritual terrain we now find ourselves living in, Christians over forty are the immigrants who ignore their children at their own peril. That's why we focused our attention on young people.

Christianity has an image problem. We can deny it, disdain it, and decry it, but the fact remains: in our culture, those of us in the church are currently perceived as caring more about ourselves than about others.

We've brought this on ourselves largely as a result of evangelicalism's successful campaign to become America's leading purveyor of religious goods and services. This means that even for Christians, *perception is reality*. And the way we're perceived, particularly by young people, is nothing short of alarming.

In each Outsider Interview we highlight something we gleaned from the book *unChristian*. In this first interview we focused on what we see as the mother of all problems—the image problem. We wanted to learn how Christians come across to non-Christians and what we can do about it. And our guests were candid with us.

The young adults we interviewed openly shared their perceptions of Christianity.
**Watch the video
"Perception or Reality"**
at OutsiderInterviews.com/KansasCity.

We're Going to Kansas City

Situated near Kansas City in the leafy suburb of Overland Park, Christ Church Anglican is not what you'd call funky, but it is definitely a church committed to connecting with outsiders. For several years they've used the Alpha program to provide outsiders a place at the table, and when I say table, I mean it quite literally. Alpha is an evangelism

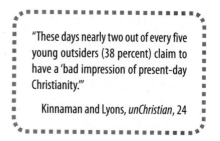

"These days nearly two out of every five young outsiders (38 percent) claim to have a 'bad impression of present-day Christianity.'"

Kinnaman and Lyons, *unChristian*, 24

23

program based on food, friendship, and authenticity. Each week small groups of friendly Christians and curious outsiders meet for dinner to discuss the meaning of Scripture and the doubts of outsiders. Alpha is one of the few evangelism programs based more on listening than talking.

The leader of the Alpha program at Christ Church is Kirk Wulff. We asked Kirk to find the guests for this interview. Amazingly, Kirk managed to get four people to agree to sit on a stage with two strangers (Todd and me) and share some of their deepest feelings about spirituality, religion, and Christianity.

Showtime

Most Christians have never seen an interview like this done in church. Of course, we've all watched Oprah, Dr. Phil, and Leno do it, but for some reason we hardly ever think of using this format in church. That fact alone can create a sense of expectation, and Christ Church Anglican was buzzing.

"Please help me welcome our guests Tony, Sarah, Klarisa, and Dan."

I asked each guest to give us a little background and playfully added, "Who talked you into doing this interview anyway?"

Sarah is a flight attendant with Southwest Airlines. Her childhood religion, Roman Catholicism, didn't stick, but after coming to Alpha with her sister, she'd become a regular attendee at Christ Church. Ironically, she is still uncomfortable with the label "Christian" for some of the same reasons outsiders talk about.

24

Dan is also an ex-Catholic and now identifies himself as an atheist. He is a friend of a friend of Kirk who agreed to do the interview at the last minute as a favor to him. Tony is a special education teacher who came to faith. In spite of his determination to never become a Christian, Tony's good friend in high school invited him to youth group, where Tony connected with Jesus in a serious way. The power of one interested person never ceases to amaze me. We're all suckers for love, kindness, and goodness. All it took was one good person, and Tony became a follower of Jesus.

Klarisa graduated from a university with a degree in nursing but soon decided that that line of work wasn't for her and took a job at Starbucks. She had been born into a Jewish home. Her parents divorced and her mom remarried. Klarisa soon found herself being raised by a hyper-religious Christian stepfather who didn't do much to engender a love for the church in her. The quote that begins this chapter belongs to her.

Wanting to help our guests get comfortable, Todd tossed what interviewers call a softball.

"Do you guys agree with Kinnaman and Lyons that when it comes to Christians' image problem, swagger is among our biggest issues?"

Tony jumped on Todd's pitch. "They think they're better than everybody else."

This wasn't coming from an outsider. Tony is a serious Christian who was talking about his perception of Christians. And that wasn't the worst of it. As the interview gained steam, we heard awful words to describe Christians. *Rude. Judgmental. Anti. Smug.*

And the statement about Christians that struck us as the most stinging of all: "They don't listen."

Our guests painted a vivid picture of what *swagger* looks like when it's dressed in religion. Unfortunately, all of us insiders knew exactly what they were talking about.

I once read about a business that stopped hiring consultants and switched to *insultants*. As we listened to Klarisa explain how much she longed to have a Christian listen to her, I understood how we could benefit from that kind of shift. Outsiders not only hold up mirrors, they also show us a map—a way forward for those who might be interested in traveling to new places in their spiritual imaginations. If we "stay in the room" long enough, they eventually tell us how to go about fixing our image problem. We often close our interviews with this question: "If you thought Christians would listen to you, what would you tell them?"

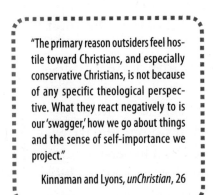

"The primary reason outsiders feel hostile toward Christians, and especially conservative Christians, is not because of any specific theological perspective. What they react negatively to is our 'swagger,' how we go about things and the sense of self-importance we project."

Kinnaman and Lyons, *unChristian*, 26

Basically we were asking them to help us become better listeners. After some nervous glances to make sure we *really wanted to know* what they thought, our outsider and insider guests told us.

"Respect *my* views."

Klarisa was obviously deeply wounded and hypersensitive to the slightest hint of judgment. But she was also quite open to anyone who would take the time to understand and respect her views, which included her Jewish heritage.

"Make a friend."

Sarah works with gay people. She loves them. She told us we should make a friend without having an agenda. Just love them, she said.

"Be *for* something."

Tony is a Christian, just not the politically correct kind. He understood that for many people being a Christian meant being against abortion, against the Democratic Party, against stem cell research, against immigration, and against same-sex marriage. He wanted to know what they were *for*.

"Read the Bible."

Dan is an atheist who assumes that a fair reading of the Bible would solve the problem for most Christians. Dan believes the most important idea in the Bible is loving others the way you would like to be loved. He thinks that if Christians learned how to read Scripture accurately, they would see this and stop being judgmental.

> "One outsider put it this way: 'Most people I meet assume that *Christian* means very conservative, entrenched in their thinking, antigay, antichoice, angry, violent, illogical, empire builders; they want to convert everyone, and they generally cannot live peacefully with anyone who doesn't believe what they believe."
>
> Kinnaman and Lyons, *unChristian*, 26

KEY LEARNINGS:
Turning Mirrors into Maps

While listening to what outsiders have to say about Christianity, it's easy to get bogged down. They can sometimes come across as being as intolerant as they accuse us of being. But if you listen and *look* carefully, a map emerges.

Here are some key learnings the three of us discovered.

Wash Your Own Face First (Todd Hunter)

On the platform at Christ Church Anglican, Tony confirmed out loud what the research in the land of outsiders uncovered: "[Christians] think they're better than everybody else." Indeed, after doing many more Outsider Interviews since Kansas City, I've heard us Christians described as bad-mannered, condemnatory, and self-righteous. "No news there," you might think. True. Here's the news: Christians do not believe they actually act in judgmental ways.

In seminary classrooms, undergraduate courses, conferences, seminars, and church congregations, I've asked crowds of Christian people a simple question. "Call to mind your Christian friends and family members. Now, do you think most of them are hypocritical judgers of others?" Consistently these groups say "No!" They say that most of their friends would never judge other people. In fact, they tell me they are more worried that Christians as a whole are losing the ability to know right from wrong and thus the impetus to judge at all.

What then are we to make of both the research and the anecdotal comments I receive? When in doubt, ask Jesus. Here, from the Sermon on the Mount, is Jesus's take on the matter:

> Don't pick on people, jump on their failures, criticize their faults—unless, of course, you want the same treatment. That critical spirit has a way of boomeranging. It's easy to see a smudge on your neighbor's face and be oblivious to the ugly sneer on your own. Do you have the nerve to say, "Let me wash your face for you," when your own face is distorted by contempt? It's this whole traveling road-show mentality all

over again, playing a holier-than-thou part instead of just living your part. Wipe that ugly sneer off your own face, and you might be fit to offer a washcloth to your neighbor. (Matt. 7:1–5)

With his characteristic brilliance, Jesus gets to a core issue I believe lies at the heart of evangelism today: *outsiders are* observing *their way into faith and followership of Jesus.* What is it exactly that they are scrutinizing? Our lives. The lives of individual Christians, small group Bible studies in the workplace, Christians who talk on cable news shows, Christian neighbors, and those who host Christian radio shows. Sadly, when outsiders see "faces distorted by contempt," they come away with the conclusion that as a group we are hypocritical and judgmental.

But this current predicament is not the end of the game. There is hope. In fact, I have seen change happening in the last few years. Christians have heard the message. They have looked in the mirror held up by the wider culture.

As I write, all over America, Christians—especially young Christians—are taking Jesus at his word. These young people did not live during the more Christian era of the 1940s to the 1980s. Nevertheless, because they are in tune with popular media, they feel the rejection of the church and Christianity by the wider culture. In response, many young followers of Jesus are practicing the self-evaluation and spiritual growth on which Jesus insists. As we Christians begin to wash our hearts, so to speak, and to focus on living lives of goodness, our faces and tone of voice will come into line. The smug contempt will disappear, having been replaced by authentic love. When that happens, evangelism comes alive. We wash our faces to pursue Christlikeness. We do not wash our faces for any utilitarian reason—like to win an argument or as a tactic to get people to come to church. That would defeat the whole purpose. Rather, we apprentices of Jesus wash our faces because it is the right thing to do according to Jesus, our Master. But we can hope that when those observing their way into faith see such washed, self-giving lives, they might be more apt to receive the washcloth held out in our hands.

Do Not Confuse Acceptance with Endorsement (Craig Spinks)

After each city's main stage interview, I guided our guests to a more private setting where I interviewed them individually (edited segments from these interviews can be found at OutsiderInterviews.com). These interviews were often more in-depth and sometimes revealed surprising twists. That was certainly the case in my interview with Klarisa. As I sought to better understand her negative perceptions of Christianity, she told me about a time when she felt abandoned by some Christian friends.

A few years back she'd become pregnant by a man she'd been dating only a short period of time. Finding herself in a moral dilemma, she asked some friends whether or not she should get an abortion. Interestingly, the friends she chose to talk with about this were Christians. As you might guess, her Christian friends told her getting an abortion was out of the question. This troubled Klarisa, because for her the decision was not as clear-cut, and she felt as though her friends were willing to put their friendship on the line if she chose to get an abortion. However, one friend was different. This friend, also a Christian, shared that she didn't think abortion was the best option but also recognized the complexity of Klarisa's decision. She said she would be there for Klarisa no matter what she chose. Klarisa ended up deciding to have an abortion, and her friend stayed true to her word; she even took Klarisa to the clinic. Klarisa's other Christian friends stopped associating with her.

I think one of the trickiest aspects of interacting with outsiders is navigating difference. Many times we're afraid that disagreement will be confused with judgment or that if we don't disagree strongly enough, our love and acceptance might be confused with endorsement. Of course, there are no simple, easy formulas for how to disagree respectfully, but as I listen to stories like Klarisa's, I wonder how much we really have to worry about love and accep- tance being misunderstood as endorsement. It was clear that Klarisa understood that her

Klarisa bravely shares about her difficult decision to have an abortion. **Watch the video "An Outsider's Difficult Choice"** at OutsiderInterviews.com/KansasCity.

friend didn't agree with her decision, yet Klarisa still chose this friend to support her during this time in her life. Klarisa's friend was somehow able to separate her difference in opinion from her love and acceptance of Klarisa. Klarisa even said that this friend's actions are the only reason why she might still be open to Christianity in the future.

We might not be able to anticipate appropriate responses to differences we encounter, and those responses may be different from situation to situation, but what we can do is try to keep in mind that love and acceptance are not forms of endorsement—they are basic human behaviors that every person deserves.

How to Get Hired as a Christian Consultant (Jim Henderson)

You may already have someone in your life who has "hired" you to be his or her Christian consultant. Here's how you can tell: they approach you privately and say something like, "Hey, did you see that TV preacher the other night? What was that all about?" or "Did you read what Pat Robertson said in the paper about the hurricane?" or "Wasn't it cool that the Dalai Lama came to town?" They're basically looking to you to explain spirituality or Christianity.

For some reason, they've decided to trust you. Maybe it's because you don't swear, or maybe it's because you do (just a little). Maybe you once let slip something about God or Jesus that sounded authentic, and they overheard you. Maybe they've been watching you for years and finally decided they would take the risk of revealing a personal struggle, or perhaps they're so lonely that they ignore the fact that you're a "fundamentalist" and talk to you anyway.

Whatever their motive, they're trying to hire you to be their Christian consultant. Here are ten things you can do to land the job.

Top Ten Practices of a Christian Consultant

1. Ask them about *their* spiritual interests.
2. Ask them what they think of Christians.
3. Ask them what they think of Jesus.
4. Ask *them* to pray for *you*.
5. Ask them what their needs are.
6. Offer to read the Bible with them (if appropriate).
7. Don't invite them to church (right away).

8. Find a way to have coffee with them.
9. Ask lots of questions.
10. Resist the urge to spiritually fix them.

In the Old Testament, God told the Israelites to take a small piece of leather and wrap the written law on their arms and around their heads (see Deut. 6:8). I'd like to suggest that you do something similar. No, not an actual piece of paper or a rubber band; that's too easy, not to mention too eccentric. Instead, choose one of the practices on this list and memorize it. Just one. As you go through each day, periodically recite that practice *out loud* to yourself. I think you'll be surprised at how the Holy Spirit will use that simple practice to increase your connections with the outsiders who surround you right where you live and work.

3

KLARISA GETS SAVED

Following Up with Kirk and Klarisa Three Years Later

Jim Henderson

I suspect that most people who read this book are trying to understand what evangelism looks like when it stops being a program and starts being a spiritual practice. For my money, Klarisa's story is the best example of this new approach to evangelism. It's not the drama (though there's plenty of that in the video); it's her transparency and the nonmanipulative intentionality that is demonstrated by Klarisa's Christian consultant, Kirk. We met Klarisa and Kirk in Kansas City.

We tell their story partly to satisfy those who ask us questions about the results of all this relationship stuff. Do people ever become Christians using your approach? Or more pointedly, does anyone ever get saved? We think if more Christians followed Kirk's example, more people like Klarisa *would* get saved.

Christians need role models and examples of what evangelism as a spiritual practice looks like. Because we've been fed program evangelism for so long, we've lost confidence in the idea that ordinary Christians can connect with non-Christians in authentic, nonmanipulative, and transparent ways. This book and these interviews are predicated on the belief that evangelism is done best when untrained, non-bold, anxious, ordinary Christians do it.

Kirk and Klarisa's story provides answers for people who are asking questions like these:

- Should I invite my friend to church?
- When do I "have the talk," aka present the gospel?
- How long should I wait before "challenging" them to make a decision?
- If I focus on one or two people and ignore others, is that okay?
- Is it possible to invite someone to follow Jesus without losing that person as a friend if they say no thanks?
- If they say yes, then what?

Many evangelism programs are designed to help you bring your non-Christian friend to a decision. In fact, the father of modern evangelism, Billy Graham, named his own magazine *Decision*. Traditional evangelism training has taught us that the big thing is for *them* to make a decision. That's what works and what gets rewarded. What if that isn't true anymore? What if we're the ones who need to make a decision?

That's what Kirk did. Before asking outsiders to make a decision to follow Christ into his world, he made a decision to follow Christ into their world. Kirk Wulff is a pastor, and as such, he is expected to spend the majority of his time in his office at the church. However, after doing some reading and reflecting, Kirk decided to make a change.

"Why was it important for me to hang out in my office at church so much of the time? Why not pick a hangout where I can actually meet people and enter into friendships and conversations with everyday people? So I started hanging out at Starbucks for the first two hours of my day while checking and writing email, doing research for talks for classes that I would be teaching, and doing other work that didn't require me to be in the office."

Pastor Kirk left the safety and predictability of his church office and moved to a local Starbucks. He treated this time as a "discipline." He assigned himself to spend the first two hours of his workday at Star-bucks the way some Christians assign themselves to read three chapters of the Bible or pray for sixty minutes each day. He stacked his books on the table, started reading, and the inter-ruptions began. By the way, Jesus was a master at turning interrup-tions into opportunities.

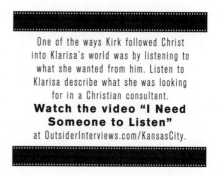

One of the ways Kirk followed Christ into Klarisa's world was by listening to what she wanted from him. Listen to Klarisa describe what she was looking for in a Christian consultant.
Watch the video "I Need Someone to Listen"
at OutsiderInterviews.com/KansasCity.

A therapist once said, "You can act your way to a new set of feelings faster than you can feel your way to a new set of actions." Kirk *decided* to stop waiting to feel convicted, guilty, or moved by the Spirit. From reading the Gospels, he understood that Jesus spent the majority of his time with out-siders. In obedience to his master's example, he took action and relocated. Instead of waiting for something dramatic, he did what was *doable*. He knew how to order coffee. He knew where to sit in Starbucks. He simply leveraged this cultural awareness and "snuck up" on the unsuspecting Starbucks crowd. He parked himself at a table for two hours, making him hard to miss and impossible for not only regular customers but also the staff to ignore.

Let's take a closer look at how Kirk used his time to connect with his new friends at Starbucks.

1. *He got to know the staff by name.* "I spent my time getting to know the staff. At Starbucks they're trained to get to know the names of their patrons. I wanted them to know that I made it just as much a priority to know their names, thus treating them like real people."

2. *He helped them.* "Whenever I would see a partner struggling to put up the umbrellas, I would go outside to help them. The barista at the register most of the time is a friendly woman named Helen in her mid-seventies. I loved to go out on a snowy day and scrape her car windshield so she wouldn't have to when she got off work at mid-morning."

3. *He made them look good.* "One time I had $50 left on my prepaid Starbucks card. It was April 16th, the end of tax season. I gave the card to one of the staff and told them to use it up buying drinks for people going through the drive-through to celebrate the end of tax day. Not only did the patrons appreciate the gift, but more importantly it gave me credibility with the staff."

One day while practicing the art of noticing people and paying attention to others, Kirk spotted Klarisa sitting at a table. She had an enormous binder full of material in front of her. Klarisa was studying for the Starbucks shift supervisor test.

"All I did was say, 'What are you looking at?' Our friendship started with that small question. I've learned that small talk is a natural on-ramp for the opportunity for deeper conversation. It wasn't long before Klarisa would come sit with me during her lunch hour. I was there to just listen to her. We talked about her work, her college experience, and everyday kinds of things. Eventually it led to deeper conversations, but I never forced or tried to steer the conversation. Frankly, I felt honored that she was willing to spend time with me during her breaks. Over time I became a trusted conversation partner. We would have deep conversations about life. She was going through some challenging life situations at that time. She seemed to appreciate having someone who would just listen and bring a different perspective. It's important that people understand that I've learned more about being a trusted conversation partner and spiritual friend from my relationship with Klarisa than I ever imagined."

We underestimate the true size of small talk. It is how people sniff each other out. We chat our way to change. That's what Klarisa was doing with Kirk. She knew he was a pastor and a Bible guy, but for some reason (such as the Holy Spirit prompting her) she decided to test him to see if he was safe.

Kirk was on Klarisa's territory, her terrain. Again, following in the footsteps of his master, Jesus, Kirk moved into *Klarisa's* neighborhood (see John 1:14 in *The Message*). In the same way Jesus and the Samaritan woman understood the rules around the town well (see John 4:1–26), Kirk and Klarisa understood the rules of socializing at Starbucks.

And just like the woman at the well did with Jesus, Klarisa began to probe to see if Kirk could be trusted as a conversation partner.

When Klarisa discovered that Kirk was the real deal, she opened up with him about her disappointments with Christians. Kirk recalls, "Klarisa had significant pain inflicted by Christians and the church, and she was willing to share those stories with me. She eventually agreed to do this Outsider Interview as a favor to me. A couple of other people I had lined up had to drop out at the last minute, so Klarisa stepped in. The reason it wasn't as challenging for me to bring these outsiders to the interview was because by that point they were my friends."

You can watch the interview and other Klarisa clips to get the full story on her issues with the church and how another Christian friend (besides Kirk) assisted her in a particularly painful period of her life.

I recently spoke with both Klarisa and Kirk and asked them to share with me what has transpired since our first interview. You can read some of those details in chapter 13, "Where Are They Now?," but here are some things that jumped out at me.

Over the course of the months following our interview, Kirk offered Klarisa a Bible, and she accepted. He then invited her to attend an Alpha group at his church. Alpha is an evangelism program based around a shared meal where people with questions about faith can come and get their questions answered in a nonjudgmental environment. I asked her why she decided to attend an Alpha group, and she said with a giggle, "I finally gave in to Kirk's pestering." I asked her why she responded to Kirk's pestering when she'd resisted other people's pestering about spiritual issues. "I knew he really cared about me as a person," she responded. Klarisa not only attended that Alpha course, she also attended two more and eventually became a key volunteer. "People gravitate to Klarisa. She's a natural discipler," Kirk shared.

About a year later she agreed to be baptized. I asked her how that experience impacted her. "I felt clean, like the slate had been wiped fresh. I used to wake up feeling depressed; now I wake up and wonder what new things are going to happen."

Kirk told me that following a recent Alpha course, a sixty-five-year-old woman who was trying to find faith asked Kirk if there was someone who could tutor her. Klarisa stepped forward. Now she and her senior friend meet weekly to discuss life, faith, and Jesus.

Klarisa is getting married soon. Her fiancé is not a believer, but he attends church with her and is very open and supportive of her spiritual journey.

Eventually word about Kirk's spiritual practice of drinking coffee and connecting with people at Starbucks got out. Now more of his fellow pastors have assigned themselves time at Starbucks to practice the art of noticing others as well.

This could become a movement.

4

THINGS CHANGE

Billy Graham's Socks and the Threat of Postmodernity

Todd Hunter

Let's practice what we've been preaching and start this chapter by listening to what our guests in Kansas City told us. Here's what I heard:

"We like Jesus's teachings . . . but Christians don't follow them."

Klarisa didn't just want Christian ideas *told* to her; she wanted Christianity *explained* to her in a *conversation*—one where she got to talk as well.

Outsiders believe the only thing Christians care about is being right and proving others wrong. They believe that in conversations with Christians there is an undercurrent of arrogance.[1]

They say they object not so much to our belief system as to what they call our *swagger*.[2]

It's stunning to see the words *arrogance* and *swagger* attached to followers of Jesus, isn't it? It would be one thing if these criticisms were at-a-distance stereotypes, but unfortunately these observations come from real-life, up-close encounters with Christians.

While I am very sure swagger is not true of all Christians, it's true enough that it is now assumed by the majority of young outsiders.[3]

The research from *unChristian* shows that:

- outsiders express their highest levels of opposition toward *evangelical* Christians,[4] and
- like a corrupted computer file or a bad photocopy, Christianity, they say, is no longer in pure form. One-quarter of outsiders say that their foremost perception of Christianity is that *the faith has changed for the worse.*[5]

By the way, before we go too far here, do you remember the quote from Klarisa at the beginning of the second chapter? *"I've never had anybody say they want to save me and felt like they truly loved me."* This sentiment captures some of what has changed over the past few decades. That's because *answers* and *decisions* as the first instincts of seekers have given way to *relationship* and *acceptance.* That's what Klarisa and the other outsiders were asking for in Kansas City—relationship.

All models and methods of evangelism spring forth from a context, an era, or a social condition. When Billy Graham was at the height of his success, there was, in comparison to today, a low level of resentment between insiders and outsiders. Can you recall someone saying, "I watched a Billy Graham

Crusade on television (or went to a stadium to hear him) and thought he was a flake"?

Arguments were employed more easily when people basically agreed with the main principles of the faith and were just looking for a nudge to make a decision. Read the words in the next paragraph. I'll bet you can-

> "Only one-third of young outsiders believe that Christians genuinely care about them (34 percent). And most Christians are oblivious to these perceptions—64 percent of Christians said they believe that outsiders would perceive their efforts as genuine."
>
> Kinnaman and Lyons,
> unChristian, 68–69

not only call to mind the right picture but also, unless you are a really young reader, hear Billy's utterly unique tone of voice. Picture and hear Billy giving an invitation to come to faith:

"You may have gone to church when you were young . . . you may have been baptized . . . you may have been confirmed . . . but tonight you know you do not have a personal relationship with Jesus Christ . . . and so I'm going to ask you to come . . . to make a decision . . ."

I am not criticizing Billy Graham—you'll see where I am going in a moment. In fact, I am such a fan of Billy Graham that good friends of mine have often teased me that if I ever got fired from my job, I'd probably end up as the curator of the Billy Graham Museum. But did you catch that last word? *Museum.* Graham has a museum dedicated to his life's work. Actually he has two: one at Wheaton College in Illinois and one in Charlotte, North Carolina. Billy is so famous, so admired and respected, that he has surpassed even being a brand. For him, personhood has turned into institution.[6]

But as great a person as Billy is—and he is a person of enormous character, gifts, ability, and integrity—he was not always an institution. He is so respected today that people have forgotten Billy Graham was a controversial risk taker as a young evangelist.

Graham, reflecting on his early years, said, "We used every modern means to catch the attention of the unconverted."[7] What were some of these attention-seeking methods? Graham and his team were known to wear "garish, neon glo-sox," argyle socks, and hand-painted ties;[8] they wore "bright suits that all the world might know Christianity to be no dreary faith."[9] And Cliff Barrows was known to be on stage with a trombone or even a "consecrated" saxophone.[10]

What in the world is a consecrated sax—and why would anyone care? Why were loud clothes or a trombone of any consequence? Here's why. In the 1940s they were all symbols of the evil of the music of the Roaring Twenties. It would have been something like being heavily pierced and tattooed a few years ago—not cool to parents and not cool to the Youth for Christ board of directors who had just hired this young Mr. Graham.

I sometimes have wondered if someone on the YFC board ever thought of firing Graham and his team for their "excesses" of attire. Just think, you might have never heard of Billy Graham—and history would have been different.

In other words, Billy did his amazing work in a setting that is different from ours. Billy spoke to crowds of people who at least knew the Sunday school stories of Zacchaeus up the tree, Jesus driving out the money changers, Jonah and the fish, and so on. That is not the case today. We can no longer assume that when most people begin to consider faith, they are thinking about making a personal decision about something that is already familiar to them.

A number of years ago, I was told by a professor of evangelism that the average person who came down to the field in a stadium to receive Christ had experienced four positive contacts with Christians or the church. About fifteen years later, another professor said that the number had grown to sixteen positive contacts before a person responded. Today, research from David Kinnaman shows that mass evangelism can often cause more negativity than positive reaction.[11]

How do we explain this? Simple: *things change.*

Cultural climates have changed in every which way over two thousand years of church history, but God has never been checkmated or rendered unable to respond lovingly. We do not need to get bogged down in a lot of history or theology. We just need to remember this: *there is no such thing as effective evangelism that is not reflective of its cultural context.*

Graham's form—and he is the archetype of many others—did not come out of the blue. It arose precisely within a context, a context that held power for most of the history of America and especially in the decades following World War II. This context was marked by two important mindsets: one, the optimism surrounding science that is inherent in modern ways of thinking; and two, a Christendom vibe—Christendom being the times and places in which Christianity and Christians are respected members of the larger society and therefore have a place at the table of power in culture. But things started to change in the 1960s and picked up steam with the cynicism following Vietnam and Watergate. Modern ways of handling truth, religion, and church have been in turmoil for the past few decades.

"Anchored to the Rock . . . Geared to the Times"

"Anchored to the Rock . . . Geared to the Times." Those two phrases comprised the slogan of Youth for Christ when Graham began doing evangelistic meetings with them. Whatever Billy did to try to relate to the inquirers at his events, whatever he did to stay geared to his times, he also had his focus squarely on keeping his message anchored to the rock of the biblical story.[12] Though Billy was the finest example of this in our lifetime, he was not the first. The Bible tells us two stories about how necessary and difficult this process of being anchored and geared can be.

The first story is that of Peter and Cornelius (see Acts 10). If you are like me, you probably think of the story as "the conversion of Cornelius and his household." I read the story that way as well until about ten years ago when I heard a friend expound on the text and show how Peter had to be "converted" before he could be used by God to bring God's grace, forgiveness, and new life to Cornelius's household. I instantly saw my friend's point and wondered why I'd never seen it before!

Think about it: Jews were not to have close fellowship with Gentiles. So being faithfully Jewish meant not doing what the vision was asking Peter to do. God had to repeat it and get a little forceful with Peter before Peter was willing to see Cornelius as "clean" and go to his house.

Paul tried to walk a similar line. Giving us a glimpse into his inner world, he said:

> I have voluntarily become a servant to any and all in order to reach a wide range of people: religious, nonreligious, meticulous moralists, loose-living immoralists, the defeated, the demoralized—whoever. I didn't take on their way of life.

I kept my bearings in Christ—but I entered their world and tried to experience things from their point of view. I've become just about every sort of servant there is in my attempts to lead those I meet into a God-saved life. I did all this because of the Message. I didn't just want to talk about it; I wanted to be in on it! (1 Cor. 9:19–23)

> ### unChristian Research
>
> The three of us have been deeply impacted by the research emerging from *unChristian*. I'm on record as having said in many cities that I think it is one of the most important evangelism and ministry books of the last decade. The facts are not for the faint of heart, and coming to terms with the implications will take courage, but we have no other option than to listen. We are the ones who are alive now. We have to deal with it—even if it scares us—for there is no risk-free way to engage the culture in a conversation about faith.

Paul didn't use the anchored/geared language, but you can hear his heart: "I entered their world. I tried to experience things from their point of view. I was geared to others, but I did not lose my bearings in Christ. I didn't take on their way of life; I stayed anchored to the rock."

Quite the tap dance, huh? Connecting with outsiders can be scary, pushing us out of our comfort zone. The reality is that *there is no risk-free way of doing evangelism*, of simultaneously staying anchored to the rock and geared to the times.

If we are to do as Paul, Peter, and Billy Graham have modeled for us, we must first ask the question, "What is different about our time, and how do we remain relevant?"

Billy came on the scene when the modern worldview went unchallenged in mainstream society. Christianity was largely respected. It certainly was not being bashed in the media. With that in mind, we can say that a partnership between the modern world and Christianity gave rise to Graham's ministry. Remember, there is no such thing as a model of evangelism that is disconnected from the culture. We could just as accurately say that a partnership between the ancient Roman world and Christianity gave rise to the rapid growth of Christianity in its early years. Roads that enabled travel, the cultural acceptance of free-flowing ideas (as long as you paid homage to Caesar), and forums for public discourse were what made the early missionary journeys possible.

What about us? What does it mean to be relevant in the early part of the twenty-first century?

The New Atheism

"What's new," you might ask, "about something as old as atheism?" The current brand is not your normal, humble, I'm-not-convinced-about-God atheism. It is down on religion and the church to a whole new degree. A succession of bestselling books have torn into religion:

- *The End of Faith* by Sam Harris
- *The God Delusion* by Richard Dawkins
- *God Is Not Great: How Religion Poisons Everything* by Christopher Hitchens

These new atheists

- condemn not just belief in God but also respect for belief in God;
- say religion is not just wrong, it is evil; thus atheistic evangelism is a moral imperative;
- assert that atheism is virtuous—as righteous and honorable as those who worked against slavery;

- seek to deliver our children from God-based falsehoods—as previous generations did when fighting against slavery or the belief that the earth was flat;
- argue that bad ideas foisted on children are moral wrongs; and
- think that unless we renounce faith, religious violence will soon bring civilization to an end.[13]

An article in *The Economist* summed up the new atheistic viewpoint well: "When historians look back at this century, they will probably see religion as 'the prime animating and destructive force in human affairs.'"[14]

I think you might agree with me that when the question changes from "Is the church cool?" to "Is the church evil?" we have a larger problem on our hands. It is one thing for "cool" to lurk beneath swagger, but it's quite another for evil to do so.

Postmodernism

The contemporary world is rife with skepticism regarding the modern, scientific, empirical worldview that was handed down to us over hundreds of years of history. Why? For many young people today, *truth* does not seem to be experientially *true*. People—especially young people—are tired of being spun, sold, lied to, and manipulated. So much so, in fact, that they wonder if there is anything that is *not* spin or hype or being forced on them.

This is not to say that proclamation or propositions or "facts" are no longer valid. It is to say that people access, hold on to, and pass on truth in a variety of ways. It is to say that in our present time relationships, community, and conversation are prized over empiricism and rationalism—even though people actually live their lives in very rational ways.

Frankly, I don't think we actually live in a postmodern world. I think we live in something even more unsettling—we live in a time between the times. A new world seems to be coming down the birth canal while the other one is not yet in the grave. As my friend Len Sweet has said, most young people today are natives to this new culture. But we older folks are strangers in a strange land—and we feel it. We feel much the way Peter and Paul must have felt. We're trying to figure out a whole new reality.

Post-Christendom

The "post" in post-Christendom points to something after Christendom. *Christendom* is a socio-historical term referring to times and places where the church has been granted status in culture. This status was first given by governments or royalty but can also be granted by pop culture, such as Billy Graham's acceptance as "America's pastor."

Christendom refers to the time when the old white steeple on the corner of First and Main in most small cities in America did not just dominate the architecture of the corner on which it sat but likely also dominated the psychology of the town.

The little town I formerly lived in, Eagle, Idaho, is an example of this. Three churches once sat within a block or two of our "First and Main." These three churches sat physically in the middle of Eagle and were respected in the culture of that small town. Now? One of those churches is a coffee shop, one is a furniture store, and the other is a secondhand shop. I'm not arguing that it is wrong to renovate the physical structure of churches. I'm simply pointing out that the past religious reality of my little town, and many others, is now gone, replaced by what some commentators call the new religion of America: consumption and commerce.

Most of us over the age of thirty can remember when the church and Christianity were respected as players at the tables of power in society. To have this status suddenly taken away, and on top of that to be told that *we're the problem*, is a difficult pill to swallow.

Klarisa's Clarion Call to Conversation

For Jim, Craig, and me, the number one takeaway from our experience in Kansas City was the confirmation of our thesis: the church can no longer proclaim the gospel from a distance and be relevant to young outsiders. Like Peter, we've got to risk getting in their lives. Some have referred to this practice as that of "presence"—we must *be with* those around us. Our personal, even physical, presence matters.

Closely connected to presence is *the persuasive evangelistic power of listening*. We need to pay attention to this for two reasons.

First, virtually every young outsider I meet has some negative, firsthand story to tell about Christians. My anecdotal research is supported by the more careful science behind *unChristian*.[15] We need to let outsiders tell these stories and listen without judgment. But don't worry: conversation means, by definition, two-way communication. If you'll let them tell their story, at some point they will usually stop and say something like, "So what do you think?" Then it is time for you to talk, to comfort, to tell your story of redemption, and so on.

Second, when we had a modern world that loved and valued experts, it gave rise to a kind of evangelism in which the experts in the church could stand on high stages and talk to masses of people. But in the midst of postmodernism and post-Christendom, the culture is calling for conversation, dialogue, and sitting on the same level.

This listening bit can be challenging. Some of us fear that "conversation" sounds too much like "compromise." But as Paul showed, we must learn the power of entering another's world.

Have you ever caught an episode of *The Tonight Show with Jay Leno* in which he was doing his "Jaywalking" segment with his microphone in hand, asking questions out on Hollywood Boulevard? Imagine Jay decides to play word association. Putting his microphone to the mouths of people on the street, he says, "Evangelicals." How many people do you think Jay would have to interview before he heard the words "really good listeners"?

Let's keep this real. We simply don't have a reputation for listening. But if our guests in Kansas City are in any way reflective of others, we need to get comfortable being uncomfortable. We need to become experts at being in conversations we don't control.

In times past we rightly assumed that people mostly listened their way into faith. That meant we played the role of the *talker*. Today seekers often *talk* their way into faith.

They tell their stories, ask their questions, make observations, and so on. That places us in the role of *hearing*, *listening*, and *connecting*. This, by the way, is why Alpha courses like the one at Christ Church work so well. When people's deepest questions and concerns are listened to in the context of Christian hospitality offered through a nice meal, friendship, teaching, and the conversation that follows, you have the ancient and future formula for effective evangelism.

Evangelism Has Gone Spiritual

Hearing, listening, and connecting must be authentic qualities of being. They cannot merely be tactics. Most everyone in our culture is both used to and sick of being sold things. They know instinctively when someone is being nice just to sell them a product or service. If hearing, listening, and connecting are mere tactics—if they are not rooted in genuine, altruistic love—they become deceitful forms of manipulation.

In other words, surprisingly, evangelism is moving away from programs and mass systems and is *going spiritual*. It is going in the direction of spiritual formation. Kinnaman and Lyons call a lack of authentic spiritual formation *unChristian* lives. Kinnaman said these unChristian lives were a major barrier to outsiders coming to faith.

Spiritual formation is now a huge doorway to faith. *Today's outsiders are looking first for what's real, not what's right*. Later they will ask "What's right?" or "What should I believe?" Listening and engaging their lives with genuineness opens doors and widens eyes, and it creates the kind of conversation in which the gospel can be openly discussed.

God Is Not Stumped!

Here's some good news: God is not stumped by the current state of affairs. He is not anxiously pacing the golden streets, saying, "Oh, myself! What am I going to do? I did not antici-pate postmodernism! Quick, Peter, do a Google search: What in my home's name are epistemology and deconstruction? Who are Foucault, Derrida, and Rorty?"

Do you think God's will is actually in jeopardy because of a few philosophers? Do you see this as a chess game in which God is trapped?

I certainly don't!

Here's what I think. Somewhere out there is a twentysome-thing man or woman (or group of men and women) who is the next Billy Graham. (Not in the way Billy was, because as stated earlier, all approaches to evangelism are contextual.)

The God *who is not stumped* is raising up young people, natives to this culture, who will create new models that prac-tice *hearing*, *listening*, and *connecting*.

5

PHOENIX OUTSIDERS

Beliefs and Blinders

Jim Henderson

This chapter is based on our Phoenix interview. To get the complete story, be sure to watch the videos online (for free!): OutsiderInterviews.com/Phoenix

When you produce events in a wide variety of churches, you learn to keep your expectations low. The host venue for this conference in Phoenix, however, was Mountain View Lutheran Church, and they were throwing our bell curve off in a serious way. They had the room prepped and the tech team ready to work. Mountain View Lutheran overwhelmed us with hospitality and a motivated cadre of volunteers.

The preshow dinner with our guests is an important part of how we prepare for each Outsider Interview. Beth Fitch had recruited all of our guests including Abdo, the only Muslim guest we interviewed in any of the cities.

My phone rang. It was Beth. "He's celebrating Ramadan, Jim." Beth wanted to give me a cultural heads up about our Muslim guest. "He's fasting, so don't offer him any food, and don't give him any money or he will be offended." (We gave the other guests $50 each.) "Oh, and he's bringing five friends with him. I hope that's okay."

"Bring 'em all, we have plenty of food," I assured Beth as I quickly scanned the food table and just as quickly remembered they'd all be fasting. "No problem, it'll be fun."

This flurry of activity is typical. Last-minute changes have now become part of the plan. Sometimes one of our guests will get cold feet. Some of them have been talked out of participating by their non-Christian friends on the drive to the venue. They are certain that their friend is walking into some kind of trap we Christians have deviously set. It's all very colorful.

A few minutes later Beth, her Muslim friend Abdo, and his entourage walked into the venue.

"Todd, meet Abdo and his friends," she said.

Todd extended his hand and, not having gotten the fasting memo, pulled them toward the food. Beth jumped in to rescue Todd from the cultural faux pas. "Hey Abdo, come over here and meet Craig. He works with Jim and Todd."

Craig sat down with Abdo and company and began to get the backstory on how Abdo got talked into doing this interview. The room was full of energy. It's always this way. Good will, curiosity, and friendship permeate the atmosphere. Helen, who was leading the concierge team that welcomes and connects people, walked in with her warm smile and an armful of materials and said, "Jim, can you guys help me get these brochures folded?" With that, all of us—interviewers, producers, outsiders, and insiders—grabbed some brochures and furiously folded as we talked, ate, and fasted.

We eventually straggled out onto the stage to continue the conversation we'd begun in the dining room. This little group that had formed less than an hour before around a common curiosity about religion, Christianity, and spirituality had already bonded.

Todd launched into the interview with a provocative question. He wanted to know how our guests felt about the strange practice we Christians have developed of calling them *lost* behind their backs. Turning to Erin, he asked, "So, have you heard that famous story about the prodigal son?"

Erin is highly educated and had spent a fair amount of time around Christians when she was in high school and college. You could tell she was working hard to connect with the story. "No, I really don't remember that story, Todd."

Looking for help, Todd turned to Abdo. "How about you, Abdo? Do you know this story?"

Abdo came up blank as well.

Having spent the past ten years asking many people this same question, I was not surprised that our outsider guests had no working knowledge of a story we insiders take for granted. For me, this brief exchange provides a snapshot of the spiritual predicament we find ourselves in. For the past five hundred years, the tectonic plates of socio-spiritual change have been slowly grinding right under our feet. Post-Christendom is no longer something that will happen in the future; it's happening now. Normally the time we "see" an earthquake is when the stuff is falling off the shelves. This awkward moment between Todd, Erin, and Abdo captured my attention in the same way.

Todd could see that Erin had more on her mind and asked her a follow-up question. "Erin, we Christians aren't trying to be mean. How did the language we meant for good come out sounding so bad?"

Erin, who during college had succumbed to being baptized in an attempt to satisfy her Christian friends, was wondering why that wasn't enough and why she needed to do something more, such as accepting Jesus as her Savior.

As I listened to Erin and Todd, I found myself wondering how the church let someone like Erin slip through our fingers. It was almost as if we had inoculated her—we'd given her just enough of Christianity to make her resistant to Jesus. Even after all the religious influences she'd experienced, she sounded about as interested in God as a lapsed member of an Elks lodge at a recruiting dinner.

This wasn't the case for our two insider guests. Brian was firmly committed to Jesus but less certain about the church. "When it comes to sharing Jesus, the church is the biggest problem," he responded when I asked him what hindered him from evangelizing. Our other insider guest, Alyssa, had just returned from a short-term missions trip to Africa where she "preached the gospel to Muslims." I watched our Muslim guest Abdo carefully to see how he was taking the news that his people were being targeted for conversion by Alyssa's people. He was gracious and took it in stride.

As the host of the interviews, I not only read our guests, I read the audience. I pay attention to body language (leaning toward or away from us?) and eye engagement (looking at us or the ceiling?). Experience has taught me that people can only stay engaged for one to two minutes before they get bored or distracted. From all of the signals, it was evident that this Mountain View audience had some questions of their own, so we handed them the mic. The first question was aimed at me.

"Jim, earlier in the interview you asked the panel if they'd heard what you called the most widely understood version of the gospel, which you suggested was 'accept Christ and you go to heaven, and if you don't, you go to hell.' Here's my question: Why did you frame the question that way? Why not ask them to respond to John 3:16, 'For God so loved the world,' instead?"

Erin's been baptized but now discovers there's more. What does it take to be in? **Watch the video "In or Out? Erin Wants to Know"** at OutsiderInterviews.com/Phoenix.

The person who asked that question is a very old friend of mine and was one of my first mentors in the faith. Ironically, he was one of the people who had impressed upon me the importance of letting people know they had to make a decision to accept or reject Christ. Fortunately, his influence in my life included more than his *Left Behind* theology. He and his wife opened their home to hundreds of young people who were coming to faith during the Jesus People days, including me. They lived sacrificially and showed us what following Jesus looks like when it's not a program. Like all of us, he has mellowed with age, which explains why he was trying to get me to reframe my question to our guests so that it sounded better. He wanted me to focus their attention more on how much God loved them and less on hell.

Without knowing it, my friend was continuing to mentor me. He was checking to see if my beliefs had morphed into blinders. Blinders are the shields racehorses wear to keep them from doing what they do naturally, which is to yield to their peripheral vision. Peripheral vision can come in handy when you're trying to avoid car wrecks or notice people sneaking up on you from the side, but if you're trying to win a race, it can take your focus off the goal. Beliefs can be like that as well. They help us stay focused, but when they become too important, they can disable us from seeing people and listening to their stories. As soon as we hear something that doesn't align with our beliefs, such as *Muslim* or *gay*, our beliefs become blinders that block people out of our view. Winning, being right, and getting the last word in become everything.

> "Most Christian young people told our interviewers that our faith seems too focused on other people's faults. More than half the young Christians between the ages of sixteen and twenty-nine (53 percent) said they believe that the label *judgmental* accurately fits present-day Christianity."
>
> Kinnaman and Lyons, *unChristian*, 182

Interestingly, following our interview, I noticed that Brian and a whole group of friends, including a young gay man from the audience who had asked about homosexuality, were heading out to have coffee and continue the conversation. Brian had enough flexibility in his beliefs to see these people as people and was secure enough in his beliefs to not be threatened by difference.

KEY LEARNINGS:
Turning Mirrors into Maps

According to sociologist Peter Berger, "language objectifies reality." In other words, sticks and stones can break my bones, and *words can really hurt me*. The words we use to describe reality have power and have an effect on how we feel about things. They certainly did with Erin. Try as she might, she couldn't understand why she was "lost" or why her sister would be going to hell. Likewise, when Christians hear words like *Muslim* and *gay*, we also have knee-jerk reactions.

Here are some key learnings the three of us discovered.

The Lost Story (Todd Hunter)

Do you enjoy telling jokes based on your favorite movie, novel, or television show? If so, you've undoubtedly had the sad experience of blank stares coming back to you from friends who have never seen your beloved show or read your pet piece of literature. You threw out beloved jewels and got zilch in return. Not even a chuckle or faint smile, just a trying-to-be-polite gaze.

Abdo and Erin gave me just such a comeuppance. I know better than to make assumptions in conversations about faith. I know most people do not pay much attention to the Bible—Christians included. But doesn't everyone know the story of the prodigal son? I mean, come on—you don't even have to know the Bible. You just need to know a little art. Rembrandt's "The Return of the Prodigal Son" is one of the most famous paintings of all time! But that logic does not seem to matter. People today barely remember the Temptations or the Beach Boys, much less Renaissance art—and even less the ancient text of Scripture.

Abdo and Erin teach us that with reference to the Bible, we live in a situation similar to a guy on a bar stool telling jokes that require someone to understand the premise and context on which the joke is based. These days it seems as if no one knows our biblical story. And in the case of the prodigal son, it is one of the most important evangelistic stories in all of Scripture. Even if I had gotten lucky and Abdo and Erin happened to have a vague knowledge of the story, I'll bet they could never connect easily with the reason for which Jesus told the story.

How are we to conduct conversations about faith when our main tool for communication, the Bible, is only going to receive blank stares and polite gazes at best, and ridicule and derision at worst?

Thinking first on the negative side, don't make my mistake: don't assume. But also don't come off as if, in your knowledge of the Bible, you have some secret information available to no one else. Don't act as if you knew Barry Gordy or Brian Wilson. See, I just did it—I just assumed and voiced information only possessed by serious fans. (For all you musical outsiders, Gordy founded Motown Records, and Wilson was the composer-genius behind the Beach Boys.)

On the positive side, try telling the biblical stories in confident, comfortable, inviting tones, the way you might tell a child the story of the Wizard of Oz or the Three Little Pigs. The Phoenix interview would have unfolded much differently had I begun with, "A man had two sons. . . ." Every ear in the place would have been tuned to me. After completing the story I could have then asked, "What do you think or feel about what you just heard?" At that point a conversation would have begun—the kind of conversation the Holy Spirit often uses to help outsiders come to faith.

Be Careful Little Mouth What You Say (Jim Henderson)

Language not only objectifies reality, it *fires it up*. Why do you think "gay" has replaced homosexual as the default term for almost everyone? That's a powerful example of how language "pushes buttons" regardless of which side you support. Now imagine what a non-Christian *feels* when they hear us insist they're "lost," "going to hell," or even something we think of as almost a technical term: a "nonbeliever."

These words are not sacrosanct. They are not Scripture, and even when they are lifted out of Scripture, it's obvious not all Christians agree on which terms to use. For example, some call the Bible "the Word of God" while others call it "Scripture." Many Christians have stopped (or never started) using the once widely popular term "born again." Instead they use "came to faith," even though "born again" is in the Bible and "came to faith" isn't. They felt free to create language that fits the culture and carries less baggage.

We need more flexibility in our language options when it comes to communicating with the people Jesus misses most, people who haven't been influenced by a Christian worldview. We also need to check our own reactions when they use words that push our buttons. Outsiders can be just as naïve as we insiders are when it comes to following the old adage "it's not what you say but what they hear" that really matters.

Who Are We to Judge? (Craig Spinks)

One of Erin's dilemmas shared in the interview is a common one. She can't imagine why someone like her sister, an outsider who has dedicated her life to serving the poor, would be sent to hell. Essentially Erin doesn't want to be a part of a religion that would exclude her sister based on what she views as unnecessary red tape. Frankly, I would love to be able to tell Erin that her sister's religious affiliation means nothing to God and that she's a shoe-in for heaven, but I don't know that. On the other hand, I also don't know that her sister will be eternally punished for failing a litmus test. I've heard many Christians say things like "No one but God knows who will enter heaven" but then turn right around and make presumptions about what characteristics aren't worthy of salvation. I doubt any of us really want the responsibility of being the ultimate judge, but let's face it, it's tempting to make guesses.

I could be completely off base here, but if someone is pursuing Christ, and it's ultimately God's call, what business do we have telling people where *we* think they're going? What if, instead of trying to answer Erin's unanswerable question, we flipped the question back to her, admitting that her guess is as good as ours? Erin may still never be interested in Christianity, but acknowledging our uncertainty could very well eliminate a pointless hurdle between her and God.

6

THE BIG QUESTION

How Did You Get Outsiders to Agree to Do This?

Jim Henderson

Here's the question we get asked most about our Outsider Interviews: "How did you get the outsiders to agree to participate?"

Even though I know this question is coming, it still catches me off guard because it exposes the not-so-hidden reality that we Christians have drifted so far away from the people Jesus misses most that we think it's difficult to find a couple of them who might be willing to talk.

Don't feel bad—even the professionals can't find them. As part of our preparation for the interviews, we asked pastors to recruit four guests, and even with six months lead time, many of them were unable to find even two outsiders who trusted them enough to get on stage with them.

The reason is simple. In order for people to trust you, they have to know you or know someone who knows you. The sad fact is that most Christians, especially professional Christians, have lost touch with outsiders.[1] Our contact with them usually only occurs if they come to our church. So if you approach people you have no real relationship with and ask them if they would like to be part of an interview you are doing with non-Christians—and oh, by the way, we actually will call you "outsiders"—it's unlikely they will say yes . . . unless you're Beth Fitch.

Beth is the person who helped us find the guests for our interview in Phoenix. Her story is a case study in what it looks like when a Christian has a natural connection with outsiders. I thought hearing how she went about it might prove helpful to those of you who are considering doing this yourself.

Beth is a lawyer and a very active follower of Jesus. She knows lots of Christians and non-Christians. She is comfortable interacting with people who are on the path toward faith as well as those who aren't. She is connected with a large network of Christians who are interested in the same thing, which is why she was able to take on this unusual assignment.

I asked Beth about her experience. "Because I know loads of outsiders, I thought it would be a no-brainer, Jim, but then you raised the bar with 'I need a Muslim between the ages of sixteen and twenty-nine.' I do know a few Muslims, but not in that age range. So I put word out to my network, and soon I was on the phone with Abdo, a young man from Yemen who is now selling cars here in Phoenix. Abdo heard about the interview through the daughter of a friend and agreed to do it as a favor to her. He was quite comfortable with the whole idea but told me that he would not be eating until after dark since it was Ramadan, plus he wanted to bring five Muslim friends along. Given all our country has gone through since 9/11, you can imagine I had some anxiety about five Muslims showing up on a church campus. It sounds weird, but I was actually afraid that some Christians might act inhospitably toward them, so I arrived early to meet them before the show and escorted them to the preshow dinner."

Beth's comment about inhospitable Christians could not have been less true about the folks at Mountain View Lutheran. They were warm and welcoming, but I understood her anxiety. As Kinnaman's research uncovered, we Christians have become so closely associated with politics that we are a bit unpredictable to outsiders.

Connectors

Beth is what I call a *connector*. Connectors might replace traditional evangelists in the coming decades. Here's why: evangelists have *speaking* skills; connectors have *listening* skills. Evangelists *win* people to Christ; connectors *woo* people to Christ. Evangelists understand *apologetics*; connectors understand *apologies*. Evangelists engage in *debates*; connectors engage in *dialogue*. Finally, evangelists count *conversions*; connectors count *conversations*.

Most significantly, Beth has learned that when it comes to connecting with people who have a skewed image of God or who have closed themselves off from God, the two most important questions are not "If you died right now, do you know for sure you'd go to heaven?" or "If you were standing before God and he said, 'Why should I let you into heaven?'

what would you say?" The two most important questions are "How are you?" and "How is your family?"

Have you noticed that you haven't been able to change your basic personality structure? You are who you are. Because of Jesus, you are hopefully a better version of yourself than you were without his help, but you still possess the same personality. Trying to become someone other than who you are is simply a waste of time. You are not me or Beth. You are you.

Since God has asked us to connect with and serve outsiders, he must be prepared to do it through each one of us in a unique way. That's what we mean by *really personal evangelism*. The only other logical conclusion available (and the one that has been the default mode for the past fifty years) is that this is a job for specialists (aka evangelists). Since that is not a biblically plausible solution and since most of us seem to retain an urge to serve and connect with outsiders, we need to find doable spiritual practices that enable us to connect with outsiders in normal ways.

For almost fifteen years, I've been experimenting with spiritual practices that enable us to connect with the people Jesus misses most. After watching Beth, Todd, Kirk, and others, I've come up with a simple list of things *you are already doing* that will lead you to connect with outsiders if you just do them a little more intentionally.

People change when you give them something to do that they are already doing. We adopt new technologies like smartphones because we already know how to use a cell phone. We adopted the cell phone because it was a portable version of something we already knew how to use, the home phone. We adopted iPods because they are a high-tech version of the Sony Walkman, which was an improved version of the

Four Things You Already Know How to Do

1. Notice People

Everything we need is right in front of us. If we look closely enough, we will see things that others don't see. My wife calls this seeing people "out of the corner of your eye." All connecting begins with noticing.[2]

"Klarisa was sitting at a table with an enormous binder full of material in front of her. I simply asked, 'What are you looking at?'"—Kirk

2. Be Curious

We long for people to be interested in us. There's something about someone inquiring into our lives and our thinking that helps us make better decisions. Being curious is a spiritual practice for Beth and Kirk.

"Klarisa said she was studying to be a shift supervisor and she needed to learn everything in the book. Our friendship started with that small question. I've learned that small talk is a natural on-ramp for the opportunity for deeper conversation."—Kirk

3. Be Intentional but Not Manipulative

When I ask people why they don't evangelize, the number one reason is that they don't like manipulating their friends. Kirk and Beth have learned the spiritual practice I call non-manipulative intentionality—which means the practice of being intentional without being manipulative.

"At the grocery store I request the 'bagger' to help me take my groceries to the car. I always engage in conversation. The first question is

usually 'How are you?' Most people don't expect you to sincerely care about the answer. When I follow up with a more in-depth question, these kids begin to really open up. I have chatted with kids in the grocery parking lot about things from school failures to dysfunctional families to friends' suicides."—Beth

4. Practice the Golden Rule

The easiest way to connect with outsiders is to practice this: Do unto others as you would have them do unto you. That one rule is the only "program" you will ever need. I estimate that upwards of 90 percent of all evangelism programs violate the Golden Rule. Here's what I mean:

Do you like being thought of as a project?

Do you like it when a friend turns out to actually be a salesperson?

Do you like being talked down to?

Do you like it when your opinion is wrong (a lot)?

Seriously, think about how simple this is. It would explain why the majority of Christians persistently stonewall evangelism programs. Perhaps they have been obeying the Spirit all this time while those of us who are paid to be Christians have been attempting to talk them into acting against Jesus's words about loving people the way you would like to be loved. What if history proves them right? Some of us think we may be on the threshold of discovering just that.

cassette player, which was a portable version of the tape recorder in our homes.

Beth is doing things you and I *already know how to do*. The only difference: she does them on purpose.

The Power of Like

The most important spiritual practice Beth has perfected is something profoundly simple but radically different. Simply put, she has moved beyond love into *like*.

Saying God loves people is easy. I like to joke that God has to love people in order to keep his job. Theologians explain it by saying his nature is love. Do you love people you don't really like all that much? We all do. But when I say I like people, I mean I admire, respect, and enjoy them. I'm interested in what they like and dislike. I enjoy their company.

Has anyone ever asked you to explain the gospel and given you about thirty seconds to do so? I started experimenting with different responses, beginning with the tried and true *God loves you* angle, but that didn't seem to impact people all that much, probably because we've said it so many times on TV, bumper stickers, and bad church signs. But when I started asking people "What if there was a God who liked you—would that be good news?" their eyes lit up. This has become my short form explanation of the gospel: *Jesus is the God who likes people*. I realize this may not satisfactorily address the issue of sin for some, but it doesn't shut down the conversation either.

Beth reminded me numerous times that she actually *likes* the outsiders with whom she connects. Beth said, "Because I am genuinely interested in hearing their stories, people open up. I also try to relate to them. If I have had an experience that is similar to their experience, I share it. This creates a bond and leads to deeper sharing by them."

Don't think for a minute that Beth doesn't care whether people become followers of Jesus—she does. Beth said, "John is my personal trainer at Lifetime Fitness. We have spent hours together and talk about everything. He was an easy choice for an outsider interview we did one Sunday morning at church. When he was in the church lobby right after the interview, one of his clients, R.J., came up to him and said he did a great job. R.J. is theologically trained. John and R.J. then began a dialogue about Christianity. John decided he would start reading the Bible but needed some direction, so he mentioned that to R.J. Now R.J. gives John Bible reading assignments and they meet to talk about the assignments. John says he still doesn't believe in organized religion and isn't interested in going to church, but he wants to know more about the Bible. John told me that he talks about the interview pretty regularly. He said it was a fantastic experience for him."

What has changed for Beth is this: while she remains passionately committed to seeing her friends become heartfelt followers of Jesus, she will not coerce, manipulate, or violate those friendships to accomplish that goal. The reason Beth can make that commitment is because she has discovered the power of *like*. Beth has discovered that *when people like each other, the rules change*.

The Backside of Like

But liking people can cut both ways. It sure did for me.

Tim and I became friends in high school. He was trying to be a Christian at the time, and I did my part to help move him in the opposite direction. I turned him on to jazz and saved him from Young Life. Following high school we both began doing what was normal for us at that time—smoking pot. Since I was a musician, this went with the territory, but I needed to keep a day job, so I limited my drug use to pot and wine. I was happy and told myself I would never shoot drugs intravenously. I liked Tim and admired his intelligence and coolness.

Tim and I shared an apartment for a while. I walked into the kitchen one afternoon just as Tim was "tying off." The meth was in the needle, and he was about to load up. I'd never seen anyone do this up close, so I watched with rapt attention. He invited me to join him, and I did. Just like that I forgot my promise to myself and followed Tim into serious drug use, just like he had followed me away from Young Life.

I ended up shooting drugs and selling them for a few months until I finally dropped it all. It was getting in the way of my ability to play music, which was of greater importance to me, so I stopped. I was fortunate I didn't get hooked.

From that point on I realized I could never again say *I would never do something* because I had proven that given the right influence, I really could.

The point I want to make is this: because I respected and admired Tim, I casually dropped what I perceived to be my deeply held beliefs, picked up the needle, and shot dope. There was no long discussion, and he never tried to coerce me. I just did it.

As we can see from watching Beth, this influence can be used for good as well as evil. That's because *when people like each other, the rules change*—for good or bad.

It turns out that Jesus can take our no-frills lives and make them effective. He can take our small efforts to connect with outsiders and multiply the meaning of them the same way he multiplied the five loaves and two fish. He doesn't need much; he just needs us to *do something on purpose*. That's all that Beth is trying to tell us. And that's all outsiders like Erin are telling us they need—someone who will notice, be curious, and not manipulate them.

They know you want them to know Jesus. That isn't what offends them. What bothers them is that we go about it in inauthentic and not-so-normal ways. What bothers them is that while preaching at them about Jesus, we fail to live like Jesus.

"Eighty-five percent of young outsiders conclude that present-day Christianity is hypocritical. Half of young churchgoers agreed that Christianity is hypocritical (47 percent)....

"Overall, 30 percent of born-again Christians admitted to at least one type of sexually inappropriate behavior in the past thirty days, including online pornography, viewing sexually explicit magazines or movies, or having sex outside of marriage, compared with 35 percent of other Americans....

"Among young outsiders, 84 percent say they personally know at least one committed Christian. Yet just 15 percent thought the lifestyles of those Christ followers were significantly different from the norm."

Kinnaman and Lyons, *unChristian*, 42, 47, 48

7

PUTTING *THE OUTSIDER INTERVIEWS* TO USE

Students Teach Their Professor

Todd Hunter

In this book Jim, Craig, and I, with reference to outsiders, strive to put faces to facts and stories to stats. In this chapter I want to take us a step further and tell you what my students learned when they read the first edition of the book. By the time you are holding this second edition in your hand, *The Outsider Interviews* will have been in print and on DVD (originally included with the book) for more than two years. In that time I have used *The Outsider Interviews* as core curriculum in undergraduate courses on communicating faith in contemporary culture, in seminary courses, in adult-education classes, and in various seminars and conferences. In addition, I have hosted live Outsider Interview events in several college campus chapels that were so packed we had to turn students away.

This body of experience has alerted me to two things. First, there is a deep hunger among young insiders to understand their generational counterparts who are outsiders. Second, sometimes professors learn the most. And we don't just learn from our students. Sometimes we learn from their parents and grandparents. On many occasions, as I've come off the platform or stage after an Outsider Interview, I've had the parents or grandparents of young adults say to me, "Thank you! After hearing this interview I finally understand my child (or grandchild)." Over the years the post-event look of relaxed, patient, and generous love I see on the faces of these parents or grandparents has given me hope that the generational war is not lost.

Communication challenges still exist, but love invigorated by understanding is winning more and more. Breaking down barriers of miscommunication and building bridges of understanding is a chief aim of this book. Evangelism cannot be effective when we assume that others know what we are talking about, when we are saying "ABC" and others hear us saying "XYZ."

Learning from Little Bee

Let me illustrate what I mean using the popular book *Little Bee* by Chris Cleave. The story focuses on a girl, about age sixteen. She is an illegal refugee in England from Nigeria. The part of the story I want you to hear takes place after she arrives in England. During a conversation about films, Little Bee describes how back in her village during the dry season, sometimes men would bring a projector, hang a sheet between trees with ropes, and thus enable the village to watch a film. There was never any soundtrack to the movies. No dialogue that could be heard. The only sound heard by the village kids was the hum of the generator and the loud call of jungle animals. Oh, one last bit of background: the only film they had was *Top Gun*. Here is how Little Bee describes it:

> This is how we learned about your world. The only film we had was called *Top Gun* and we watched it five times. I remember the first time we saw it, the boys in my village were excited because they thought it was going to be a film about a gun, but it was not a film about a gun. It was a film about a man who had to travel everywhere very fast, sometimes on a motorbike and sometimes in an aeroplane that he flew himself, and sometimes upside down. We discussed this, the children in my village, and we decided two things: *one*, that the film should really be called *The Man Who Was in a Great Hurry*, and *two*, that the moral of the film was that he should get up earlier so that he would not have to rush to fit everything into his day, instead of lying in bed with the woman with blond hair that we called *The Stay-in-Bed Woman*.[1]

I don't know about you, but I can discern some other morals from that movie. Tom Cruise's character was more than just in a hurry. The "Stay-in-Bed Woman" was there for a reason!

All too often, as Little Bee illustrates, we're just guessing at what is going on, and we do not understand our outsider counterparts any more than they comprehend us. Because this book seeks to facilitate conversations about faith and followership of Jesus, I want to now turn to sharing with you what I have learned from my students about faith conversations.

My Way or the Highway

During a class discussion after viewing one of the clips from *The Outsider Interviews* DVD, a student commented to me that "My way or the highway," as an effort to control a conversation, does not work well when trying to engage someone in a conversation. Rather, he said, he noticed that being open in one's mind and heart to what others have to say is crucial. He said he noticed "People are willing to talk, if only you will let them do so." This is, of course, true. While outsiders may be skeptical about listening to us, they are often willing to talk if we are willing to listen to them. We've said similar things throughout this book. But here I want to make a specific statement about why Christians have a hard time listening: we've been taught that we *own* the highway and that we *control* and *govern* the flow of it like state highway troopers.

I'm not sure the church ever had that much influence in the world, but we thought we did. Today, however, to do well in evangelism, we need to slip comfortably into some other, more modest metaphors.

Salt, Light, Yeast, and a Mustard Seed

I've got a proposal to make. I think the conversation between the church and the world would go much better and be more rich and honest if we took Jesus at his word about how the kingdom of God, the expressed intent of God, comes to pass on the earth. Jesus's metaphors for the fulfillment of God's purposes were surprisingly modest. He spoke of salt, light, yeast, and mustard seeds. Salt, because it is readily accessible, has no economic value, but it keeps food from going bad. Yeast is similar to salt in that it doesn't cost much, but without it bread does not rise. A mustard seed is tiny, but it grows into a large shrub. The lights of Jesus's day were modest as well, but even the smallest flickers of light have the power to show us where we are, to orient us to reality—like the very real chair on which we would stub our toe without the candle's light. Let me tell you a story that illustrates the enormous power of a modest bit of light.

One night, while I was leading the evening service of a Southern California megachurch, all the lights suddenly went off. In an instant we were sitting in a blackout. The neighborhood electrical grids had failed due to an automobile accident. Thousands of people filled the main room. Our precious children—many hundreds of them—were in a large area behind the sanctuary.

Sitting in the front row of the church, I was only steps from the hallway leading to the children. It was hard to move. The dark was so disquieting, overpowering, and disorienting that it felt like a *Man vs Wild* effort to feel my way to the door. Finally pushing open the door into the hallway, which was hundreds of feet long, I noticed that a mom—of course!— had beat me to the door on the other end of the hallway and had found the small flashlight on her keychain in her purse. Now she was like a mama bear making her way to her cubs.

Her small light did not illuminate the whole hallway—not even close. But it did reorient the whole frightening ordeal for me. Soon others were doing the same thing with emergency flashlights in the classrooms, and others pulled their cars up to the outside windows, shining them through the smoke-colored glass that encased the building. The kids were safe. No one got hurt.

The drama lasted only a few moments. As I made it back into the sanctuary, it looked like a sixties rock concert with all the Baby Boomers getting out lighters and waving them around as if the Beatles were playing "Hey Jude." Who knew so many churchgoers used lighters! As amusing as that scene was, what has stuck in my heart and mind for twenty years is the enormous power of that mom's flashlight to bring hope and orientation to a seriously unnerving moment.

All of Jesus's humble metaphors have a similar effect when put to use in confident faith, but faith requires we give up control and stop acting like highway patrol officers. Can you go there? Can you give it up for the sake of helping others come to faith? Can you do the little you are able to do, even if it seems to only be a tiny light (or, these days, an app on your phone)?

Knowing Does Not Exclude Others

Knowing is possible. It's weird that such a thing would even need to be said, right? You must believe in knowing or you wouldn't be reading a book. I must believe too or I would not be writing. I only write something because I want you to know it. But these days, when the topic is spiritual, moral, or religious issues, we are not allowed to know much. You can *believe* anything. Just don't claim to *know* it.

At a recent Outsider Interview, a young guest said she believed that "god" was whatever you believed him to be. Whatever god you created with your belief became your god, and he then took care of you. She said with sincerity and a straight face that her god was Santa Claus. No one laughed at her or even challenged her. But try saying that you know God answers your prayers or that you know Jesus rose from the dead with the same certainty that you know George Washington was the first president of the United States of America.

This is what I need you to know: you don't have to give up on knowing to be a good conversation partner. Without the possibility of knowing, of understanding, there is no content to discuss and thus no point for any conversation—even about where to have dinner. If *where* has no meaning, if the diner on the corner only exists in my mind, if it is only *my* truth—if dinner only means what it means to me—we are in trouble.

Thankfully, that is not the case. Language, for all its slipperiness and imprecision, and even given the fact that it is used by sin-filled human beings, still has the capacity to convey truth from the most basic of ideas to the most complex concept one might find in a philosophical article or a medical journal. It is possible for a doctor to both *know* and *love*, to *understand* and *serve*, at the same time. I know—I've experienced it. Maybe you have too.

The Christian Bubble

The undergraduates I teach attend a Christian university. Many of them have attended Christian schools their whole lives. Others were homeschooled by Christian parents. I have no quarrel with either of those facts. I just want you to know that context so you can understand what I learned next. One evening after an Outsider Interview clip was finished, a young lady in class blurted out, "I can't believe people think these things about us!" She genuinely had no idea that most outsiders had low views of the church and religion. With loving parents and dedicated teachers, her religious life had been great. I didn't mean to burst her bubble, but an interesting conversation did ensue.

For the next thirty minutes, her classmates told the stories of the upbringings they experienced in their homes and schools. No story we heard was as positive as hers. When the class fell silent she said, "In hindsight, I get it." She continued, "People have personal histories that have become filters through which they see, understand, and interact with the world. Everything we do or say affects those around us. Every person is insecure and wants to be accepted, heard, and legitimized. When I fail, when I don't even try to understand their experiences, I only further harm, hurt, or abuse them."

This girl was not dumb or even particularly naïve. Like all of us, she only saw through the lens of her honest experience. What she learned that night in class was not primarily cognitive or intellectual. It was more in the heart, the gut. She was learning to deal with people on their terms. She was learning that she and her honest viewpoint were only fifty percent of a conversation.

Tolerance: An Act of Love

These days when we use the word *tolerance*, we tend to associate it with the notions of pluralism and concepts linked to relativism. Tolerance has become a code word of sorts. In casual conversation today it normally means, "Don't judge me, my actions, my words, or my attitudes." The thought is that since there is no objective truth, such judgments can only come from partial and personal points of view, and thus such judgments have no validity for others. If the judgment is effective and valid for anyone, it is effective only for the holder of the judgment.

I get it. I have genuine empathy for those who think in those ways. Mean-spirited people wielding words that do damage have abused a large part of our population, but "leave me alone" is a very meager and weak understanding of tolerance. As followers of Jesus we can do much better.

Tolerance, rightly understood, is an act of love, generosity, and hospitality. Tolerance does not demand that someone enter the conversation with us the way we wish they were. It accepts others as they are—really. The ancient Jews, trapped in captivity, did not want to be *tolerated* by a vague god of their own making. No, having believed in a personal Creator God, with whom they were in covenant, they were looking for the one true God, their precise and concrete God, to come save them and deliver them.

African Americans living under the horror of rank racism during the twentieth-century Civil Rights era were not looking to be *tolerated*. They were looking for a generous, hospitable love from those in power, those who made the rules of exclusion from schools, certain workplaces, and specific public spaces. Black people were hoping, rightly, to be accepted as full human beings on par with any person of any color. It seems so obvious *now*.

But don't miss the irony here: we cannot defeat racism—we cannot banish it from the human condition—without truth. If there is no truth, but only one's view of things, then the human race is doomed to "isms" even more evil than racism.

Thankfully, in Christ we can have our cake and eat it too. We can—we must—hang on to truth. And we can do so with a tolerance that does not merely leave our neighbors to do, think, and say as they please. That may be tolerance in the popular mind, but Christians are shooting for something much higher. We aim for faith, hope, and love . . . and the greatest of these is not tolerance but positive love—love that seeks the good of others always, even to our own detriment.

That is an evangelistic best practice for any place and any time. Put it together with the other lessons my students taught me, and you, as an insider, can be on your way to being an appropriate and fruit-bearing conversation partner with outsiders.

8

DENVER OUTSIDERS

Diversity and Difference

Jim Henderson

This chapter is based on our Denver interview. To get the complete story, be sure to watch the videos online (for free!): OutsiderInterviews.com/Denver.

Kathy Escobar and Karl Wheeler lead The Refuge, a missionally inclined faith community in Denver. A couple years ago Kathy, Karl, and several carloads of Refuge-ites caravaned over to Seattle to experience a conference I'd put together called Off The Map. They loved it and asked if we could do something similar in Denver. We said yes! Kathy and Karl are highly respected in the Denver area and asked Foothills Community Church to sign on as cohosts for the conference

87

there. We even had a few celebrities (at least to us) at the Denver interview: David Kinnaman, whose book *unChristian* originally inspired us; Matt Casper, my atheist coauthor of *Jim and Casper Go to Church*; and Isaac, the lead singer of the Fray, who happened to be in town hanging out with David.

The interview started much like the others, with the guests introducing themselves and giving some background on their religious upbringing. But this interview took on a life of its own as one of our guests, Rio, began to unpack her fascinating and painful story of "coming out" as a gay person at a Christian university. Her unabashed way of articulating a deeply personal issue disarmed both the audience and me. Think about it: When was the last time you sat on stage in a roomful of complete strangers and explained your sexuality? Her enthusiastic personality left me thinking, "If you hadn't told us you were gay, we'd be thinking that you were the most 'on fire' Christian on this stage."

> "A majority of born-again Christians, including more than four out of five evangelicals, say that homosexual relations between two consenting adults should be illegal."
>
> Kinnaman and Lyons, *unChristian*, 94

I was glad that Rio was a part of our interview. Her story is one that I think all Christians need to hear. Rio described how some students at her Christian university had threatened to rape her in order to straighten her out and how others had put bullet holes through her apartment window. Her own parents effectively disowned her. While Rio's experiences may be more dramatic than the norm, they aren't as rare as you might think. Many people in the lesbian, gay, bisexual, and transgender (LGBT) community have stories of judgmental Christians.

As Rio was telling her story, I was watching Andrew, who, given his impressive résumé with Child Evangelism Fellowship, came across as a more conservative Christian. I was impressed with his ability to stay connected with Rio even when her story took a sharp turn. In many ways I think Andrew represents the feelings of many young evangelicals: settled in their beliefs but activist in their faith. I was very impressed with Andrew's ability to model what it looks like for him to hold his beliefs and still stay in relationship with those who disagree with him.

It seems to me that when people with deeply held differences, like Rio and Andrew, attempt to communicate, debate often ensues. Christians call it "defending the faith," which is often code for intellectual holy war. What if, instead of defending the faith, we chose to "defend the space"—the sacred space God gives us when we enter into relationship with *people of difference*—people who think, feel, and act differently than we do? This is why we decided to mix outsiders and insiders together. We wanted to see what happens, especially among young people, when differences show up.

Another outsider, Sam, brought the issue of immigration into focus. His unique path into and out of Christianity was colored by his Hispanic roots and his parents' involvement in full-time ministry. His explanation that his father "chose ministry over me" was difficult to hear and helped provide

> "Out of twenty attributes that we assessed, both positive and negative, as they related to Christianity, the perception of being antihomosexual was at the top of the list. More than nine out of ten Mosaic and Buster outsiders (91 percent) said 'antihomosexual' accurately describes present-day Christianity."
>
> Kinnaman and Lyons,
> *unChristian*, 92–93

context for some of the bad choices Sam made when he was younger. His self-description as a "non-Christian Christian" humorously captured his resistance to labels. He impressed me with his intelligence and nuanced way of seeing himself as part of the Christian story while not being a Christian. Sam's multifaceted story expressed something we kept running into: many of today's outsiders began as insiders, meaning that for more and more outsiders, their journey begins inside the church.

Alex did not start in the church. In fact, her parents landed somewhere between neutral and New Age, neither of which proved sufficient to satisfy her desire for a personal god. Sounding eerily similar to the biblical story of the three wise men, Alex's conversion to Jesus by shooting star was pretty cool, and were it not for Rio's coming out in public, Alex would have been the most controversial person on stage.

All in all, the biggest takeaway from our Denver interview was how respectfully the guests interacted with each other. Their body language was pretty open, and they worked at supporting each other. Sam could have been more dominant, but he chose instead to be direct without being overbearing. Andrew may have said it best when he described the difference between disagreeing with someone in theory versus seeing them face-to-face. I've discovered that when two people like Rio and Andrew appreciate, respect, and like each other, the rules change. We don't have to defend the faith; we begin defending the sacred space between us.

It's not just Sam—many insiders we talked with feel hesitant about using the word *Christian* to describe themselves.
Watch the video
"The Christian Label"
at OutsiderInterviews.com/Denver.

KEY LEARNINGS:
Turning Mirrors into Maps

In order to grasp the nuance of this interview, you need to see and hear the people—their faces, gestures, and tone of voice. If you want to see the most hopeful future of Christianity, study Andrew and Alex and listen carefully to Rio and Sam.

Here are some key learnings the three of us discovered.

Catch People Doing the Right Thing (Jim Henderson)

The drama of Rio's story is moving. It's powerful. The problem is that most of us are not like the people who put bullet holes in her window. Most of us are not like the people who tried to scare her by threatening to rape her. We may like to watch drama, but we don't like to live it. We actually live fairly ordinary lives. Most of us live lives that are more like Andrew's or Alex's. While I was moved by Rio, I was schooled by Andrew. While I was impressed with Sam, I was instructed by Alex. Unfortunately, Christians have become *addicted to drama and allergic to the ordinary*. Consequently, we can miss what's going on right in front of us. Here are a couple of things I learned when I looked closely at how our two insiders interacted in the Denver interview.

Change comes faster than it used to. Big changes used to come at wider intervals. They took time to spread and establish themselves in society. For example, there was an almost twenty-year gap between World War II and the Vietnam War. Now wars are constant and neverending. Alex and Andrew's

> "Our research shows that one-third of gays and lesbians attend church regularly, across a wide spectrum of denominations and backgrounds, including Catholic, mainline, nonmainline, and nondenominational churches. Most gays and lesbians in America align themselves with Christianity, and one-sixth have beliefs that qualify them as born-again Christians."
>
> Kinnaman and Lyons, *unChristian*, 97–98

pragmatic views of Christianity illustrated an acceptance and anticipation of this reality of change. They didn't spend a lot of time talking about the way things "should" be. They were more focused on the way things "could" be.

Diversity is normal. Having Sam share the complications of what it was like to be raised in a family that immigrated to the United States set the stage for Alex and Andrew to articulate an acceptance of this new reality in America. For them, it's common to have close friends who are from different countries, are people of color, or are gay. Even though Andrew is more conservative in his Christian views than Alex is, he did not deviate in his support of respecting gay people even while disagreeing with them. Both of them embraced diversity as part of the new reality in spite of having different beliefs.

Christians are not monolithic in their beliefs. Theologically speaking, Alex was very liberal and Andrew was very conservative, yet they were remarkably respectful of each other's views about God. This patchwork approach to faith can be seen as either a threat or an invitation. One thing is for sure: it's not going to change anytime soon. There's a lot of movement going on internally as Christianity reforms and reshapes itself in our lifetime. Alex and Andrew showed what it looks like to be poles apart without becoming polarized.

I Am Not a Leading Heterosexual and You Are Not Your Sexuality (Todd Hunter)

It happens in every generation. One sin is singled out, and if you commit it, you are reduced to it. Sometimes the name-calling is accusatory and meant to put you in your place as a sinner. When I was a kid, such a statement might have gone like this: "You are an adulterer!" or "You are a pot smoker!"

Other times the statement is meant as a way to brag about one's hip evolution into certain unapproved behavior. Thus, James Dean was cool when he was a "rebel without a cause." Katy Perry's "I Kissed a Girl" and Lady Gaga's "Born This Way" function in the same way today. Ongoing sexual experimentation is to our time what drug use and *Easy Rider* were to the sixties. Several bands in the sixties sang songs bragging about how enlightened people should celebrate drug use, while making fun of those parents, teachers, and politicians who saw drug use

Young adults often sidestep polarization by being openhanded with their convictions.
**Watch the video
"Remaining Open"**
at OutsiderInterviews.com/Denver.

differently. Jimi Hendrix, Janis Joplin, and Jim Morrison, each of whom died of a drug overdose, took the experiment a bit too far. I wonder if the "God Hates Fags" people, if they were around then, would have gone to the funerals of those three cultural icons holding placards that announced, "Crazy hippies got what they deserved!"

Let's get real here. Every thoughtful Christian I know is completely embarrassed by our initial reaction to the AIDS crisis and to modern homosexuality. Too many of us thought, "Well, you only catch AIDS if you do such and such with your body parts," as if that made all those deaths reasonable.

While we may not have confessed enough both to our ignorance and to our judgmental attitude, it is right to say that the thinking of the vast majority of Christians has evolved over the past three decades. But even if the church were to confess fully and be fully forgiven by the homosexual community, we would still have an uneasy relationship with each other. On the church's side, we tend to reduce people to their sexual practices. On the side of homosexuals, they tend to reduce those who disagree with them to "haters."

Interestingly, we don't seem to have the same uneasy relationship with those who swear and curse at people, or those who are guilty of unmistakable overconsumption of worldly goods, or those who watch objectionable television or movies. The Bible is as loud on those types of sin as it is on sex.

I believe God has views on and cares about sexual practices. I am old-fashioned enough to believe that when it comes to sex, there is both a *right* and a *wrong*. It seems to me that 99 percent of human beings on the earth would agree with me on that, although many would disagree as to what constitutes that right and wrong. Everyone is drawing a line somewhere on the continuum of sexual morality. The same homosexuals who accuse the church of rejecting them then turn and reject each other. There are some things you just cannot do in the homosexual community with impunity. Do this or that and you will be excluded or marginalized. The same is true of every community that is organized around the same sexual point of view.

Why is this line of thought important? How does it lead to a key learning for evangelism? If fruitful faith conversations are going to occur between Christians and the LGBT community, the reducing of people to their sexuality must stop.

Regarding human sexuality, that is evangelistic key learning number one: just stop it.

Rio was not our *homosexual*. She was our *guest*. I don't know what she does with her body parts. She did not say. But I do know this: she cannot be reduced to it. I know I would not want to be known as a "leading heterosexual." I am more than what I do with my body. During the vast majority of my life, I love, believe, belong, and work without any thought about my sexual orientation. I am confident Rio would have said the same thing if asked.

Like a beautiful and multifaceted diamond, Rio has many sides to her. Faith conversations work best when they start with and are attached to a facet in which you can easily find common ground. When an outsider is seeking and you are guiding, there are lots of interesting things to talk about besides sex. Unless you or they feel that an outsider's sexuality is the main barrier to them having faith (similar to the rich young ruler's issues with money in the Gospel accounts), talk about other things. Let trust, mutual respect, and love grow. In time, if a seeker's love and devotion to God grows, God will help them deal with all of their sexual issues, just like he is helping you deal with yours.

How to Stop Being Labeled a Hater (Craig Spinks)

After the hardback release of *The Outsider Interviews*, my father-in-law invited me to visit his men's group. They were reading the book as a group. I quickly discovered that the book's discussion of homosexuality was what stirred them the most, and the topic quickly became the subject of our conversation. The group is made up of middle-aged professionals who for the most part regard homosexuality as a sin, but they don't want their views to be interpreted as hatred. Their big question: What steps can they take to improve relations between Christianity and the LGBT community? I didn't have many suggestions at the time, but I've come up with a few since.

First, I think the single most helpful thing you can do is enter natural friendships with men and women who are gay. If you don't already interact with gay folks on a regular basis, put yourself in situations where you will. A while back, my wife and I realized that an increasing number of our friends are gay. It certainly wasn't something we were intentional about, but I think we somehow communicated that our interest in them went far beyond their sexuality. We are friends because we like each other. One of the biggest surprises along the way has been how grateful our LGBT friends have been for our friendship. "Supportive straight Christian" is a complete oxymoron in gay circles, but it doesn't have to be.

Second, it might help to show your cards. The perception that Christians are haters is pretty strong in the gay community. On the other hand, many Christians are terrified of being labeled a hater. If this is you, talk about it! Ask how they've experienced hatred in the past and if there's anything you've done that has communicated anything less than love to them. Ask lots of questions, and don't be afraid to admit your naïveté on the subject. Ask when they realized they were gay, how they came out, and about their experiences with Christians (they will certainly have some stories to share). When I started hanging more in LGBT circles, I was a little nervous about how my indecisiveness on the topic would be received. I really don't see that it's any of my business to determine whether or not homosexuality is a sin. I'm pretty supportive of friends who believe that it isn't a sin as well as of friends who do and are seeking change. It doesn't seem that my opinions (or lack thereof) are as important to my gay friends as the fact that I want to be around them and that I'm not seeking to change them, which leads me to my final suggestion.

Be sure that your actions line up with your words. Don't just say that you "love" them, show them! Go out of your way to be a part of their lives, go to their parties, or volunteer with them on their own turf. If your purpose for extending friendship and love is to change them, they will smell it a mile away.

Realistically, your efforts may seem like a lost cause, at least for now. The perception, true or not, that Christians are haters is strong. But that doesn't mean that we can't slowly help mend the rift one relationship at a time.

GETTING PAST GAY

Climbing the Mountain of Difference with Dad

Craig Spinks

"I'm afraid I'm not going to say what you want me to say, Craig."

Even over the phone I could tell my dad was concerned about his visit to Colorado. I'd invited him out so that we could have some face-to-face conversations as part of my research for *The Outsider Interviews*. His visit was just a few days away, and the realities were starting to kick in.

"Here's the deal, Dad: I'm not looking for you to say anything. I just want the two of us to explore what it might look like to talk about faith, especially the parts we disagree about. I guess I'm intrigued to see if we could do that without it turning into an argument."

I'd never really seen my dad nervous like this before. I can only imagine that it'd be pretty intimidating to have your son initiate a conversation about getting along better.

Then my dad popped *the* question: "Are you going to make me talk about homosexuality?"

Looking Back

I was raised in southwest Ohio in an evangelical Christian home. My parents divorced when I was eleven, and shortly thereafter my brother and I chose to live with my dad, who was and still is deeply committed to his traditional faith. Living in a testosterone-filled household provided plenty of opportunities to see my dad in good times and in bad, but somehow he managed to model Christianity in a positive light. Ultimately, he is the reason I became a Christ-follower. He was always challenging me to think about life as it related to faith, and he talked openly about his own beliefs. This was all in addition to making sure we were active in our church.

Our relationship started to change after I turned twenty and began asking questions about my faith. I realized that most of what I believed was based on things I had been taught, and I wasn't sure if I really owned those beliefs for myself. I started a process I now call "recycling my faith," where I pressed the reset button and started over. I kept some beliefs and discarded others, but I primarily reshaped the things I'd been taught to better reflect my personal experience with God. I call this recycling because I didn't just discard the faith I grew up with; rather, I reused and redeemed parts of it so that it could be useful in my life today. I began to trust myself and Jesus a little more and what I'd been taught a little less.

Naturally, some of my beliefs started to diverge from my dad's. When these new differences arose, I spoke up and defended my position. We both cared a lot about our respective

Getting Past Gay

positions, so it seemed that the more transparent I was, the more we argued. After a year or two and a number of painful arguments, I started to question the benefit of talking with my dad about these issues. When it came to things we were likely to disagree about, maybe we all would be better off if I kept my mouth shut—which is ultimately what I did. When he'd bring up something I disagreed with, I'd bite my tongue and keep quiet. The arguing stopped, but so did our conversations about faith.

Well, not entirely. We still have spiritual conversations, but they are usually about stuff we know we'll agree on and actually not very relevant to my current spiritual journey. Even when safe opportunities present themselves, I find myself steering us away from anything close to my heart. I guess I'm afraid of being hurt—not that my dad has ever directly tried to hurt me with his words, but when we argue I usually end up feeling hurt in some way. I'm like most people, I suppose: the closer the topic is to my heart, the more it hurts when the conversation turns into a fight.

A Hopeful Sign

When my dad asked if I would make him talk about homosexuality, I thought, *Oh boy, what am I getting myself into?*

"Yeah, that's a possibility," I responded. "But I don't see us coming to any conclusions about that topic. I just want to explore whether it's possible for us to talk about something like homosexuality without it resulting in an anger-filled, intellectual debate."

Dad moved on. "I watched your video of Rio the other night."

In preparation for our conversations, I'd given Dad a few assignments that included reading David Kinnaman and Gabe Lyons's *unChristian* and watching a short clip from my one-on-one interview with Rio in Denver. I was interested to see how my dad would respond to Rio talking about her struggle with homosexuality.

"Well, Craig, I have to admit, I've never heard a homosexual talk about how they've struggled with the idea of being gay, let alone talk about ways they've tried to stop. In most interviews I've seen with gays, they seem hyper-sure of themselves. It feels to me as if they want to shove their lifestyle in our faces by parading their relationships and complaining about not having equal rights."

It seemed that Rio's transparency, vulnerability, and humility had earned some points with Dad. He understood that Rio currently considers herself gay, but it mattered to him that at one time she didn't want that for herself and tried to avoid it. I exhaled a sigh of relief, encouraged by my dad's ability to listen to Rio. Maybe it would be possible for us to have a civil conversation despite our differences. Still a little gun-shy, I told my dad that we'd talk more about this when he was in town. After a few more minutes talking about the rest of the family, we wrapped up the conversation.

See the video Craig sent to his dad before his visit.
Watch the video "Rio's Story"
at OutsiderInterviews.com/Denver.

My hope for *The Outsider Interviews* has always been that it would help parents like my dad better understand their kids. In many ways our relationship captures the dilemma more and more Christian parents are experiencing with their adult children. What better way to try to overcome our differences than for my dad and me to have a real conversation? My dad's visit seemed like a great idea a couple months ago, but it turns out that the idea of dialogue is easier in theory than in practice. Each conversation I had with my dad about this project brought overwhelming feelings of anxiety, fear of rejection, and shame. I vacillated between being hopeful and hopeless. I had been hopeless, so our phone conversation brought some well-needed feelings of confidence about my dad's upcoming trip.

Missing Dad

I had been missing my dad's involvement in my spiritual life—not the arguments and debates, but the everyday conversations we had in my teenage years. I'm able to have these conversations with other people; why can't I have them with my dad? While this project is not the most natural approach, it has allowed us to be very intentional about reclaiming this aspect of our relationship, and that was the reason for my dad's visit to Colorado.

As my wife Sara and I prepared for his visit, we contemplated whether to stash some things out of sight: half-empty bottles of liquor; our DVD collection, which includes a number of controversial films; and books that he would think contained questionable theological viewpoints. I used to be more cautious about what was within sight around my dad, but this time was different. I wanted to let my dad see the version of me who is alive with passion instead of the candy-coated version I sometimes present. A part of that "real me" is in the movies I watch, the books I read, and the people I have drinks with.

What was I afraid of losing? Respect, for starters. In all honesty, I'm a "words of affirmation" junkie. I've consistently had people in my life who have been incredibly affirming and encouraging. Without them, I don't know where I'd be. My dad is my number one fan, always rooting from the sidelines. In my darkest hours, he's been at my side. Perhaps that's why it hurts so much when we disagree. Maybe I feel like his affirmation is sometimes conditional. It's not that I think we should always agree, I just want to feel as though he accepts me even if he disagrees with me.

Tense Dinner Conversation

My dad's flight arrived an hour late due to bad weather. This was ironic because I take every chance I get to rub in Colorado's great weather with my dad, who still lives in Cincinnati. Since he would be in town for just a couple of days, I had a short window of time to prove Colorado's beauty, and, well, we weren't off to a good start.

He got the first shot in. "Great weather, Craig."

"Yeah, we shipped it in especially for you," I said as we hugged and then headed for baggage claim.

We caught up while driving from the airport to downtown Denver. Sara was along for the ride and would be joining us for the weekend's activities. It was comforting to have her there, not just for her perspective in our conversations but also because I knew Dad and I would be on our best behavior with her in the room.

Dad was buying us dinner that night (an offer we never refuse) and had picked a restaurant he remembered from a childhood trip to Denver. As soon as I walked through the doors, I understood why he liked this place. Every square inch of wall space was filled with mounted heads of elk, deer, bear, and bison. My dad, an avid hunter, must have felt like he was at Disneyland. I couldn't help but think that if I ever have a cruel desire to torture my vegetarian friends, this is where I'll bring them. We all ordered steak.

As I ate, my jaw started to clench. Each bite brought more nervousness. At some point we needed to get down to business, and I wasn't sure how to make that happen without it feeling unnatural. Luckily, I can always count on Dad to bring up controversial topics. I don't know if he does it because he's unabashedly honest or if he likes getting a rise out of me, but tonight I was grateful for his brashness, whatever the motive. "Craig, I hate to be a downer, but I just don't see things getting any better for America. With this recession and the moral decline, I just see us heading on the same path as Rome."

"Seriously?" It took me a couple minutes to wrap my head around what my dad was saying. "So are you saying that you think that America is less moral today than it was in the sixties and seventies?"

"Absolutely. If someone were to have told me in the seventies that Americans, even some Christians, would be accepting of homosexuality and abortion, I wouldn't have believed it."

As Dad continued to make his point, I began to realize that he and I have very different ideas of what morality looks like.[1] In his mind, the acceptance of homosexuality is a clear indication of moral decline, while I think being more loving and accepting of the gay community is a sign of less hatred and judgment. Dad sees the world crumbling down; I see it improving.

Remembering my commitment to keeping it real, I responded, "I actually see a lot of hope in our world today. I see young people wanting to make the world a better place. I see the world becoming smaller and working together with a little more unity, and young Christians becoming spiritually awakened rather than blindly adhering to religion."

Dad was glad to hear that people my age are optimistic, but he couldn't share my enthusiasm. After politely listening, he continued to tick off the signs of moral decline and the inevitable destruction of the earth. I felt like he was channeling Pat Robertson, Hal Lindsey, and James Dobson all at once. I wanted to share about how I see the return of Jesus as being less about the earth's destruction and more about restoring earth to its original intent, but the more my dad talked, the angrier I got. This wasn't heading where I wanted it to. We were falling back into our old patterns. My dad didn't seem to be very interested in my point of view, and I was bottling up anger and about to explode. But before I could say something I'd later regret, we were saved by jetlag catching up with my dad. We left a tip and headed home to get a good night's rest.

Picking Our Way through Rocks and Boulders

Things looked better the next morning. It was sixty degrees and sunny outside, and I didn't have to start the day apologizing for something I said the night before. Maybe a new day would bring new understanding between us. "I'm glad you'll get to experience some real Colorado weather while you're here!" I said, ribbing him.

"Yeah, yeah. What do you think I should wear on our hike?"

106

My dad introduced my brother and me to hiking growing up. While other families were going to the beach, we were hiking to the bottom of the Grand Canyon. In my adult years, that has transitioned into yearly mountain-climbing expeditions as a family. We've bagged a number of state high points, including Rainier in Washington, Hood in Oregon, Whitney in California, and the list goes on. These trips have been where Dad and I have had our best and worst moments.

Thirty minutes later, Dad, Sara, and I were hiking in the foothills of Boulder County. After the previous night's challenges, I was reluctant to start up the conversation, but Dad kicked it off nicely. "Craig, the other day on the phone you asked me to think of some questions for you." He pulled a piece of paper out of his pocket and carefully unfolded it. I was nervous but glad he had taken the time to think through some questions. He continued, "Okay, here's my first question: Why do you have such a problem with church?"

For some reason this question made me realize that most of our conversations of late have been focused on hot-button issues, and we'd never really talked broadly about my journey of recycling my faith, so I took this opportunity to share a bit of that with him. It was a long answer to a simple question, but I eventually got back on track. "I don't have a problem with church, nor do I think it is a waste of time, but the traditional expressions of church just don't work for me the way they used to. The benefits of going to church I see are for connection with a community of Christians as well as having regular encouragement in spiritual growth. While many people find this in the context of a church, I've found it elsewhere in settings that are more natural for me."

Dad had more questions. It felt good having him take the initiative—less complicated. "Okay, so what else have you recycled, Craig?"

"Frankly, Dad, a lot of my beliefs and practices are being reshaped. For example, you taught me methods for how to pray, and through those methods I began to experience what I call communion with God. I think being in communion with God is what prayer is all about. Along the way I started to notice that I was also finding communion with God in ways I wasn't taught, for instance while hiking or listening to music. Since these methods are more natural for me, I've ended up counting that as prayer and not relying on the traditional methods as much."

"Does that mean that you think structure and tradition are pointless?" he asked with a slight tinge of disappointment.

"Not at all! That structure and tradition helped me get to where I am today, but at times I feel the structure gets valued more than what the structure holds up. For instance, I feel like the act of praying is valued more than the connection with God that happens when you pray. I've seen people in the church who are more concerned about upholding the structures of religion than having a relationship with our Creator. If I were to have a problem with church, that would be it."

The conversation came to a natural break as we pulled out our water bottles and trail mix and enjoyed the scenery for a few minutes. But since I was on a mission, not just a hike, I took the initiative and started the conversation back up, referring to my brother's perspective.

"Hey, Dad, when I told Dan about this project, he said it was pointless for the two of us to talk about things we disagree on. The way he sees it, you just want to change me, and I just want to change you. What do you think about that?"

After a brief pause he replied, "Well, yeah, up until the point when you became an adult, it was my job to shape you into a good Christian. I felt such a relief after you moved out because I didn't have that pressure anymore. It's your responsibility now."

While I would have objected at age seventeen or eighteen, what my dad said actually made some sense to me. In my teenage years I was independent and resistant to my dad imposing values on me, but as the prospect of having my own kids draws closer, I'm now wondering how Sara and I will handle this. I'm sure Dad would prefer I'd think and act more like him today, but from what he was saying, he no longer felt a pressure or duty to change me. I, on the other hand, had recently realized that I had not let my dad go. I realized that I had some confessing of my own to do.

"Dad, I've thought a lot about what Dan said, and I think he was right about me. I do want to change you. It's funny—I can talk with all kinds of people with whom I disagree, not caring whether or not we ultimately agree. But when it comes to you, I guess I care a little more. I really don't want to be the kind of person who imposes his beliefs on others, so I'm going to try really hard to respect your opinions more and to not try to change them.

"While I'm at it, I've wanted to talk with you about a few other things. I've made some assumptions about what you believe and have embraced stereotypes rather than really trying to understand you. I'm sorry; you deserve better than that. I've also said and done some things purely to get a rise out of you."

"You mean like the time you used the f-word?" Dad was recalling a situation a few years back when some bottled-up anger got released in the form of profanity.

"Yeah, that's a good example. The only reason I said that was really just to tick you off. Again, I'm sorry about that, but it exposes a deeper issue. A lot of times I'll avoid talking about something controversial with you until the point when I explode. When that happens I feel like an idiot because not only do I treat you poorly, but I also misrepresent the thing that originally upset me. I really want to learn how to open up before exploding, but I need something in return, Dad. I need to know that even though you and I may disagree, you will always accept me."

Dad looked me in the eye. "Craig, I am so proud of you. Nothing you could say or do would ever keep me from accepting you. You need to know that."

An awkward sense of closeness settled over the two of us. *So this is what it's supposed to feel like*, I remember thinking. We picked our way through the rocks and small boulders as we made our way back to the car in silence. On the drive back home, we picked up a pizza at a local favorite, Beau Jo's Pizza, and brought it home with us.

Failing Bridges

As the three of us were busy canceling out the calories burned on the hike, I walked over to the TV and put a copy of *The Outsider Interviews* into the DVD player. The hike was completed, but my mission wasn't. One of the reasons behind my desire for peaceful conversations is that I'd like to be able to include my dad in the things I'm most passionate about.

Currently those passions overlap a lot with the things we disagree about. Many of the views presented in *The Outsider Interviews* fit into this category, so I thought watching a few clips would be a good way to see if we were any closer to communicating better. I started with the main segment from Kansas City. As Klarisa and Sarah recounted their bad experiences with Christians, my dad grabbed the remote and pressed the pause button multiple times, the way people who are anxious repeatedly push the walk button at a crosswalk.

"That's not fair, Craig. Christians are overwhelmingly kind and loving, and all these people are talking about is their bad experiences. Surely the evangelism experiences they are talking about are with wackos. I know many people who came to faith because of the Four Spiritual Laws."

"How old are those people, Dad?"

"Forties, fifties. Why?"

I pulled out my laptop and clicked on a photo of the "Bridge to Nowhere" that Todd and Jim use to illustrate how things have changed. "Dad, this is a real photo of a bridge that at one point in time was extremely useful; it helped people cross a river. But a hurricane came through and changed the course of the river so that now it no longer flows under the bridge. The bridge is no longer useful. That bridge is like our evangelism methods; they were useful at one point in time, but the river has moved."

Sara chimed in. "Christians *are* loving, but every single one of my coworkers has talked to me at one time or another about their bad experiences with Christians or the church. And when I used the Four Spiritual Laws in college with the college ministry I was a part of, people just weren't receptive. They hated it. And so did I!"

"How old are your coworkers, Sara?" Dad asked.

"Mostly Craig's and my age—late twenties."

I added, "People tend to remember bad experiences more than positive ones. So even though a lot of positive things are happening in Christianity, that's not what we are known for. What we learned from the book *unChristian* is that Christianity has an overwhelmingly negative reputation among outsiders."

I could tell that something was starting to click for my dad as he responded. "They showed a video clip at church a while back asking people what they thought of Christianity and comparing that to what they thought of Jesus. People responded negatively to Christianity, but positively to Jesus."

"Yeah, there are even books out about that phenomenon," I replied.[2] "But let's keep rolling through these clips, Dad. We've got to head for the airport pretty soon."

We finished up Kansas City and moved to Denver. I didn't plan to save talking about homosexuality until the end of Dad's trip, but that's what ended up happening. The clip I'd sent before Dad's visit was of Rio's interview offstage with me; we were now watching the main interview, which triggered some new thoughts for Dad.

Just a few seconds into the segment where Rio comes out about her homosexuality, Dad was once again attacking the defenseless pause button. "It's absolutely absurd for her to use the words *Christian* and *gay* in the same sentence. The Bible is absolutely clear that homosexuality is wrong."

"So you don't think that someone who is gay can be a Christian?"

"Absolutely not, just like I don't think someone who is addicted to drugs can be a Christian."

112

"Really?" I was surprised by Dad's certainty.

"Yeah, if someone embraces behavior that is sinful, I don't think that person has really dedicated their life to Christ. They are choosing a lifestyle of sin over a Christian lifestyle. You can't have it both ways."

"But using your example," Sara chimed in, "it's often hard or even impossible for someone to stop using drugs."

"True, but Christians with a drug problem acknowledge that drug use is bad and are trying to stop, whereas the gay community isn't trying to get better. They say that it isn't a sin even though the Bible clearly says it is. That's the difference for me. If someone who is addicted to drugs was saying that drug use is okay and that they're a Christian, I'd say the same thing—they're not."

I get a little sensitive when it comes to people defining who's in and who's out; my tone began to reflect this. "But Dad, many homosexuals don't read those verses the same way as you. Do you think those in the gay community who call themselves Christians really believe that it's *not a sin*, or do you think it's just a cover-up?"

"Oh, I think they believe they're not sinning, but they're wrong. Craig, this is one topic we are never going to see eye to eye on."

That was one thing we could agree about. No matter how much we talked about this, not much was going to change in our interaction on the homosexuality issue. Mercifully, it was time for us to head for the airport.

As we pulled up to the airport and said our good-byes, I wanted to try one more time to get my dad to understand, but I knew that would have to wait for another day. We parted like two respectful, and perhaps wiser, sparring partners.

On the Way Home

As Sara and I headed back home, she asked me to remind her why I wanted to be able to talk to my dad about these things. "It's not so much that I want to talk with my dad about homosexuality," I said. "I just want to be able to talk about tough topics as they come up rather than avoiding them. I like hearing his viewpoints. They challenge my thinking. That's really what's behind this whole attempt to connect with him."

After gazing out the window for a couple of minutes, Sara circled back. "I guess I understand wanting to hear different perspectives, but why do you want this from your dad, of all people?"

"I've thought about that a lot, and honestly I'm not really sure. Maybe I'm just looking for his approval. But deep down I feel like our relationship has been disconnected the past couple years, and I think that learning how to navigate our differences will ultimately improve our relationship as a whole."

"But what are you looking for from your dad? What do you need from him?"

"Well, for starters I need to feel like he's not dismissing my views simply because they are different from his. I need to know that he loves me and doesn't judge me—I need him to tell me not just with his words but also with his actions. It felt amazing today when he told me that he accepted me no matter what. Now I just need his actions to communicate this. A huge piece of this for me is listening. I just want him to listen to my perspectives and maybe even show some curiosity about my viewpoint before jumping to his counterarguments."

My wife was on a mission to get to the bottom of what motivated me.

"Craig, if you were to put yourself in your dad's shoes, what would you have done differently? More to the point, what do you think we should do differently when we have kids ourselves?"

"Well, I don't think my dad did such a bad job. I hope I haven't been too hard on him. Let's face it, the question isn't *if* we're going to screw up our kids, it's *how*! But one thing I do think we should do differently is to teach our kids how to explore faith rather than adopt a set of beliefs. I want to help them process through why something is good or bad so they own the choice themselves. I wonder how my conversations with my dad might be different today if, for instance, instead of telling me all the reasons why homosexuality is bad, he asked me about why I wrestle with the issue. That way he'd be joining me in a journey rather than trying to be the tour guide."

As Sara and I drove westward toward the beautiful Rockies, we talked about ways we might approach parenting some-day—a topic we find both scary and exciting.

I'd love to end this chapter by saying my dad and I now had a perfect relationship, but that wouldn't be true. I was sure my dad and I would continue to get into arguments and say things we'd regret, but I also thought we had taken some steps in the right direction.

At some point in the not-too-distant future, I felt sure, the rubber would hit the road. A conversation would arise that wasn't part of a research project, and a referee might not be in the room. Since I'd now resigned from trying to change my dad, the only person I had left to work on was me! The real issue wasn't my dad's communication skills but whether I would be able to be more respectful of his views. Would we communicate acceptance despite our differences, or would we fall back into our well-traveled ruts of difference? I may have been naïve, but I hoped my dad and I would continue to forge a new relationship marked by mutual respect and acceptance.

Time would tell.

10

THE RISKY BUSINESS OF ENGAGING DIFFERENCE

How a Good Intention Turned into a Lost Relationship

Craig Spinks

As Jim, Todd, and I wrote the first edition of this book, I found myself identifying more with the outsiders we interviewed than the insiders. I wasn't gay and had never had an abortion, yet those were the stories with which I most resonated. This affinity is what prompted the writing of the previous chapter. I didn't want to offer commentaries on others' stories without also putting the theories into practice in my own life. I expected the writing experience with my dad to be a good excuse to work on our relationship during a nonvolatile time and hoped readers would find the resulting chapter helpful in their own relationships. What I wasn't expecting was for it to also trigger a series of events that would have me identifying more with outsiders than ever.

It all started when my dad's mom, my grandmother, received a copy of *The Outsider Interviews*. Instead of using the book for its intended purpose, to help insiders and outsiders better connect, my grandmother used it as a source for information about my beliefs. For reasons that are still unclear to me, she became convinced that I was hell bound and an evangelist for Satan. She proceeded to warn family members of my blasphemy. After the initial shock (I was always her model grandson) and hurt (Why didn't she talk with me first?) subsided, I gave her a call. Over the course of two phone conversations, I tried to reason with her, since much of her information was incorrect, and to dialogue with her, trying to understand where she was coming from. Unfortunately, I ultimately fell back into the well-traveled rut of debate, defensively arguing my case. By the end of the second conversation she asked that I never again "pollute her Jesus" by visiting or calling. I reluctantly agreed. That was the last conversation we had before she died less than a year later.

The loss of my grandma, both in relationship and in life, has not been easy for me. She was the only grandparent I really knew. In many ways she was like a mother to me, having played a significant role in my early adolescence. I loved her deeply and know she also loved me. It was difficult for me to understand how she was willing to lose our relationship, but I complied. I made one small exception after hearing of her failing health by sending a card in which I wrote, "I love you." And I still love her.

The Fallout with Dad

I honestly expected my dad to have some empathy for me after hearing how my grandma responded to the book. After all, he'd experienced her strong opinions and wild exaggerations firsthand since childhood. Instead, he aligned himself almost completely with her and used the opportunity to voice his own concerns about my life. I got the feeling that he saw this as an opportunity to double down and try to change the things he didn't like about me. As often happens in our debates, my dad started attacking what I viewed to be a straw man. In my last conversation with my grandmother I used three bad words (one of which was the f-bomb). Rather than discussing the situation in its entirety, my dad focused on these three words. He concluded that my use of those words signaled a lack of love and respect for my grandma. An ultimatum was given, though not explicitly: apologize to your grandmother, or there is no point in us continuing to talk. I didn't feel as though I could apologize in good conscience, so I didn't. My dad and I have not talked to each other in over a year.

Heroes and Villains

I bet many people reading this book can relate to my story. The details may be different, but the pain is the same. Perhaps you can relate to my grandmother's and dad's good intentions and relentless love for me. Or maybe you've been in my shoes before, a young adult relearning how to interact with his family after coming of age. Depending on your perspective, you may have already picked a side and started vilifying the other. If there's one thing I want to communicate more than anything, it's that I don't see this as a story of heroes and villains. Of course I tend to disagree with my grandmother's and dad's actions, but I can understand why they did what they did. If I were in their shoes, I might have reacted similarly. It's natural to identify with some characters in a story more than others. But when you take sides, it's easy to start viewing one side as all good and the other as all bad.

For a long time I was angered by how seemingly easy it was for my dad to lose contact with me. What kind of a father disowns his son for not behaving or believing a certain way? After a while I started to realize how unfair statements like that last one are to my father. I'm pretty sure he doesn't feel as though he disowned me. From his perspective it was probably over more than behavior or beliefs, and it couldn't have been easy. I can choose to vilify my dad, or I can try to view him in a way that honors the complexity of his situation. I'm trying to do the latter.

Woulda Coulda Shoulda

I'm now at peace about what happened, but that doesn't negate the emotional roller coaster of the past year. At first all I felt was pain—deep, deep pain. Then came anger and bitterness. After a while some positive memories started to surface. I've missed having Dad around while working on home renovations. Some of my best memories with Dad have occurred while working on house projects.

Most days I feel an odd mix of sadness, anger, and regret. I don't replay the scenario in my head as much as I used to, but it's easy to wonder *what if*. Most of my *what if*s have focused on how my response could have been different. At the top of that list is whether or not I should have apologized for using profanity. In hindsight, I don't regret feeling hurt by what Grandma said or for getting angry as a result. I do regret using profanity as a part of that anger; I knew this would push Grandma's buttons and hurt her. At the time I didn't apologize because I couldn't separate the pain and anger from the retaliation. I felt as though I was being asked to apologize for being hurt and angry, which was something I wasn't willing to do.

There are a million other *what if* questions, but after a certain point these questions can hinder any hope of progress. The past is what it is. All I can do now is put one foot in front of the other in pursuit of my own healing.

What I Learned

I don't pretend to know how to avoid or overcome situations like the one I encountered with my family. I mean, come on, my story doesn't exactly have a happy ending. However, I have been working hard to improve how I interact with people when we have a disagreement. Perhaps some of these things I've been processing might be helpful in your own situations.

Don't let assumptions overtake reality. One thing that bothered me more than anything was how misunderstood I felt. It seemed as though my dad's and grandma's assumptions about me were misguiding their actions. When I flip the situation around, I can see how I was making my own assumptions about them. When we project our own ideas onto someone or something, we don't have to go through the messy process of seeking understanding. I don't think we want to make assumptions or are even always aware of it when we do. It's a survival tool. If we didn't make some assumptions in life, we would live in a constant state of confusion. But when we let assumptions take the front seat in these interactions, we tend, as Brian McLaren likes to say, "to compare our best with their worst." I wish that I had tried to recognize the assumptions I was making and then had chosen not to let those assumptions influence my actions. Perhaps my family would have felt more understood or even respected. I know I would have appreciated this same gesture from them.

Decide how honest you are willing to be and which conversations you are willing to have. I wish I had been a bit more discerning about the things I discussed with my dad and grandma. On one hand, I wanted them to see and accept me for who I am. On the other hand, I knew that if I was completely honest, they would probably no longer consider me a Christian. So I walked a tightrope. I tried to share enough without sharing too much. In the process, I found myself trying to control their opinions of me. I now realize that I can't control how others view me; I can only control how I respond to those views. In some situations I wish I'd been more forthright and accepted their opinions of me for what they are: their own opinions.

When Grandma told me in one of our phone conversations that I was going to hell, I wish I could have embraced the idea that I'm valuable no matter what anyone else thinks. No matter how much her comments hurt, they don't define who I am. I also wish that I had been able to stop conversations I wasn't willing to have. When my dad brought up topics I wasn't comfortable discussing, I wish I had said something like "I'm sorry, but I really can't have that conversation right now." But I didn't do those things. Instead, I tried to earn their approval and control their views of me. Maybe if I were a little less concerned about pleasing them, I would have responded a bit better when they disapproved.

Be aware of how much relational leverage you use. Relationships are powerful. When a good friend gives me advice, I take him or her seriously. It may not end up affecting what I actually do, but the advice of a close friend or family member often carries much more weight than a stranger's. While I think this is an important aspect of many healthy relationships, it is also a form of power that can easily be used inappropriately. Relationships can be used as collateral to get another person to do what you want. This is what I call *relational leverage*. Using relational leverage may be appropriate in some situations. For instance, if I knew someone was planning to harm a child, I'd probably use whatever kind of leverage I could. Extremes aside, I question whether this kind of leverage is helpful, regardless of how effective it can be. Do you really want people to make important life decisions because they are pressured into them? Wouldn't you prefer that they actually make these kinds of decisions on their own?

Life can go on, even without closure. One of the most common comments I hear after sharing my story goes something like "Don't worry, someday you'll reunite with your dad." While I appreciate the sentiment, I've become quite comfortable with how my story is unresolved. In fact, I'd even go so far as to say that I think the pursuit of closure is one of the main reasons my dad and I no longer speak to each other. As I see it, both my dad and I wanted closure, and in our minds that could only happen one of two ways. We could end our relationship, or one of us could compromise our values. Neither of us was willing to compromise our values, but we both wanted closure. So we chose to end our relationship.

There was, of course, a third way. We could have figured out a way to move forward without resolution. I wish that I had given that third way more of a chance. I could have tried calling my dad after a while and said something like "Look, we both probably said and did things that we regret. We're not going to resolve this, but we can move on. I still love you, and I'm willing to give it a shot." Then, as awkward as it may have been, I could have switched gears and asked how he was doing. I haven't been ready to do that since this all began, and it could still be some time before I am ready to take that risk. If and when that happens, I hope that I am better equipped to navigate difference without the need for resolution.

Handling Hardship

Honestly, even if I followed my own advice, I'm doubtful that the outcome would have been much different. I do, however, think that our interactions would have been a bit healthier and perhaps not as painful. My goal isn't to eliminate pain or hardship in my life, but I'd like to be able to handle those situations in a more healthy way when they do happen. Ironically, I've become much more optimistic this past year. This painful experience has challenged me to work on related issues in other areas of my life, and the results have been encouraging. Perhaps someday this growth and healing may circle back around and affect my relationship with my dad. I'll just have to wait and see.

SEATTLE OUTSIDERS

The Great Agreement

Jim Henderson

This chapter is based on our Seattle interview. To get the complete story, be sure to watch the videos online (for free!): OutsiderInterviews.com/Seattle.

Don't invite me to church—invite me to serve.

Audrey

We presented our final Outsider Interview in Seattle, home of some of the most innovative companies in America. Microsoft, Eddie Bauer, Starbucks, Boeing, Amazon, Real Networks, and the Experience Music Project all call Seattle home.

125

One of the organizations I lead has hosted an annual conference in Seattle every year since 2001. We've built up a fairly strong following, as well as a significant team of volunteers who help us "put on the show." We conducted the final interview on the second day of the conference. It was great to have our team and all the musicians we've worked with over the years on site.

On this Outsider Interviews tour we ended up partnering with Anglican, missional, Lutheran, and Assembly of God churches. Calvary, a historic Assembly of God church, hosted this Outsider Interview. Forty years ago this was one of the most revolutionary churches in Seattle. They had a great deal of influence on me as a young Christian, so it was something like a homecoming for me. I was anxious to return the blessing this church had once bestowed on me.

As was mentioned earlier, for our money the most significant thing Kinnaman and Lyons discovered wasn't the difference between outsiders and insiders but rather the startling similarities these groups share, which may help explain why, regardless of the issue we raised, we couldn't get our guests in Seattle to disagree about anything. That's why instead of "The Great Debate," we called this chapter "The Great Agreement."

Recruiters "R" Us

Because I'm from Seattle, I have a lot of friends there. I asked them to help me find some interesting insiders and outsiders for this interview. Jeff, a math coach and grad student at Seattle University, invited Audrey, a fellow student, to be a guest on our show.

Steve Lewis is very connected with both insiders and outsiders. He leads The Purple Door, a kind of Christian rooming house situated right across the street from the University of Washington. That's where we found Charlie. Charlie is an incredibly bright atheist. He not only hangs out with Steve, he actually rents a room from him. The night of the interview, a group of Christian

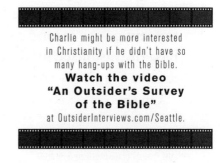

Charlie might be more interested in Christianity if he didn't have so many hang-ups with the Bible.
Watch the video
"An Outsider's Survey of the Bible"
at OutsiderInterviews.com/Seattle.

students showed up to cheer Charlie on as he attempted to help Christians understand things from his point of view.

Elizabeth Chapin began volunteering for our events several years ago. I asked her to help us find a young insider who had opinions but wasn't *mean*. Elizabeth had gone to church with a young woman named Chandra at Overlake Christian, a megachurch across the lake from Seattle. Chandra jumped at the chance and agreed to be a guest on our show. (Besides being a heartfelt follower of Jesus, Chandra is an international jump rope champion. No lie.)

My last call was to Jim Caldwell, one of the regional directors for Young Life in the Seattle area. Jim and I are not what you would call close friends, but we hang out with many of the same people, which is almost a better way of getting to know someone. Jim is one of those guys I would want to have on my side if I had to be in a street fight. He has "I've got your back" written all over him.

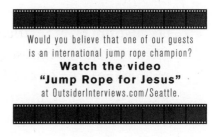

Would you believe that one of our guests is an international jump rope champion?
Watch the video
"Jump Rope for Jesus"
at OutsiderInterviews.com/Seattle.

Unfortunately, a couple insiders we had lined up to do the interview dropped out at the last minute, so I called Jim the day of and asked if he knew anyone who could go onstage without any prep. He told me he had just the guy. His name was Matt.

Matt was raised in Texas but had obviously spent a lot of time in Seattle. Wearing a knit cap, khakis, and sandals, he could have been confused with a member of Pearl Jam. His "Beyond Malibu" T-shirt didn't do much to cover up his affiliation with Young Life, which he described in a typical Seattle way as a local nonprofit.

After getting our guests situated onstage and properly introduced to the Seattle audience, we dove right into the deep end and asked if they thought Christianity had gotten too cozy with politics. The outsiders said what you would expect, but not the insiders—they didn't spend one minute defending Christianity's involvement in politics. Charlie captured their sentiments best: "Christianity is a *brand* that has become associated with one particular political party."

Our guests also surprised us with their opinions on issues from the veracity of the Bible to the philosophical construct known as *certainty*. I was certain of one thing: the sensitive topics and virtual lovefest of viewpoints was causing some of

> "Among the evangelical segment, only a slight majority are registered Republicans (59 percent). That's a high proportion, but far removed from the monolithic levels one might expect based on media pronouncements or the expectations of Christian leaders. We are projecting, for instance, that in the 2008 election, as many born-again Christians (including both evangelicals and nonevangelicals) will cast a ballot as registered Democrats as will vote as Republicans. Party affiliation does not always translate directly to candidate choice, but it is a reminder that the Christian community is more diverse, less cohesive, and less unified than is typically assumed."
>
> Kinnaman and Lyons, *unChristian*, 160

the older saints in the audience concern. Most of them had committed to memory "come out from among them, and be ye separate" (2 Cor. 6:17 KJV) by the age of six, so all this Kumbaya between Christians and non-Christians, between outsiders and insiders, was making them uncomfortable.

Todd likes to help Christians like these old saints navigate this anxiety by explaining something he calls "centered-set faith." It comes from social set theory, developed by Dr. Paul Hiebert, and it suggests that human beings tend to organize themselves in one of three ways: fuzzy sets, centered sets, and bounded sets. We're only concerned with the bounded and centered sets.[1]

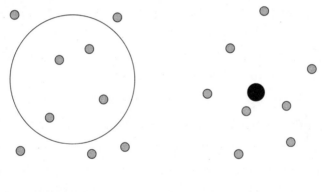

Bounded Set   **Centered Set**

In bounded sets, the main focus is on the boundary, on answering the question "Who's in and who's out?" As far back as I can remember, evangelicals have used bounded-set thinking. Conversely, centered-set thinking asks, "Who's moving toward the center, and who's moving away from the center?" This group of young outsiders and insiders was definitely centered setters. They were inclusive (some would say) to a fault. Audrey captured the spirit of this interview group with the statement "Don't invite me to church—invite me to serve." Even a follower of Jesus would have to say amen to that.

- -

KEY LEARNINGS:
Turning Mirrors into Maps
- -

Todd's centered-set faith is a helpful mental model but a challenging real-life model. It was Jesus's comfort with the centered-set life that ultimately got him killed by bounded-set devotees. Growing as a person, and particularly as a follower of Jesus, will really stretch a person. Watch the interview and see who stretches you.

Here are some key learnings the three of us discovered.

Move with the Movers (Todd Hunter)

Many practices of evangelism often spend too much time trying to motivate the unmotivated and to gain the interest of the uninterested. It is better to move with those who are already moving, seeking, questioning, and being curious. This, I think, is the big takeaway from Paul Hiebert's work on social-set theory.

When it comes to who's in and who's out, in most cases it is really hard to tell the difference—because most people are a mixture of good and bad and a jumble of belief and unbelief. Unlike God, we simply do not have all the facts on the matter. And, to paraphrase Jesus, we've all got a good-sized telephone pole in our own eye while trying to judge the speck of dust in someone else's eye.

On the other hand, who is interested can often be more clear and obvious. You can simply notice, pay attention, listen, and observe. You may not have considered it before, but for Jim, Craig, and me those four behaviors in the previous sentence are core practices for contemporary evangelism. They represent four major practices we learned doing the Outsiders project. We hope all our readers will begin to engage with them.

Perhaps the most unifying force among today's young adults is a passion for service. **Watch the video "The Urge to Serve"** at OutsiderInterviews.com/Seattle.

As always, Jesus shows us the way. Had Jesus not noticed Zacchaeus up the tree, we would have never heard of Zacchaeus. He would have never come down from the tree to have dinner and a faith conversation with Jesus. Jesus did not focus on the fact that Zacchaeus was "out"; he just latched on to Zacchaeus's curiosity and movement toward him, seen in the effort he made in climbing the tree to see Jesus as he walked through town.

If Jesus hadn't paid attention to tax collectors, we never would have heard of Levi, who became Matthew. If Jesus didn't listen, we would never have met the woman at the well. If Jesus did not observe the people in his life, we never would have known of Nicodemus. In each case Jesus does not focus merely on the *out-ness* of these people. Rather, some little movement in each of them alerts Jesus to their potential to become his follower.

These are the most simple, doable, and powerful practices we have: listen, observe, pay attention, and notice. Do so with one ear attuned to God as well. Then lovingly and humbly do whatever he tells you to do. Have someone over for dinner.

Go to an outsider's house for a party. Talk to a person in public. It's all good. It all matters. It all counts. It lends an evangelistic hand to those who are presently outsiders but are moving toward Jesus.

If You Have a New World, You Need a New Church (Jim Henderson)

For those who didn't get the "things have changed" memo, watch the Seattle interview video, and it will become crystal clear that things have changed both in the world and in the church. The only question is this: Will we change with them? Here are a few changes I've made in my thinking after interacting with our insider and outsider guests in Seattle. I thought that they might prove helpful to you as well.

STOP US/THEM THINKING AND START THINKING US

Human beings resist being preached at or talked down to. We're most open when we're treated with dignity and respect. We don't like parental, patronizing, or contrived talk. Traditional evangelism requires a teacher and a student—an us and a them. We've become experts at making people feel like outsiders. We need to find common ground with people, we need to become co-sufferers, and we need to admit what we don't know. We need to find the issues that make all humans hurt (including ourselves) and start the conversation there.

RENOUNCE BEING CONVERSIONISTIC AND EMBRACE CONVERSIONISM

I openly identify as being a *conversionist*, meaning I believe that changing one's mind about cereal, cars, music, politics, or—for the sake of our project—Christ is natural and human. What I'm not is *conversionistic*, meaning I will not violate our relationship in my zeal to get you to join my sports team or my religion. I stop claiming that I can objectively "prove" that my beliefs are real, and instead I openly embrace mystery. I invite those with other views to do the same. I stop pretending that I'm neutral. I admit my biases and encourage others to admit the same. I lead with my life. I host the conversation but refuse to control it. I challenge my own assumptions and invite others to challenge theirs. This shifts the nature of our interaction from debate to dialogue.

THE LIFE COUNTS MORE THAN THE TALK

Anyone who has raised teenagers knows about "the talk." Whole industries of advice givers abound regarding when, how, and where to talk to your kids about sex. Parents nevertheless continue to make it up as they go, pass it off to their spouse, or more often simply let others educate their kids. It's amazing how similar this is to how we approach evangelism. Most evangelism training fixates on "the talk" or "the gospel presentation." Evangelism experts tell us when, where, and how to give "the talk." We, the evangelism amateurs, like parents of teenagers, feel inadequate, underinformed, and ill prepared, so we avoid giving the talk and let others handle it for us. How about this revolutionary idea: in the same way kids learn about sex by watching their parents' love life or lack thereof, see if your non-Christian friends can learn about Jesus by watching your spiritual life or lack thereof. Any talk you give will be more like a soundtrack to a movie—it adds a lot, but it's not the movie. Your spiritual life counts for more than your spiritual talk.

Uncertainty in Disguise (Craig Spinks)

I relate closely to how Audrey describes her religious status as a lack of certainty. It's not an uncommon view; uncertainty appears to be increasingly valued among young people. What happens when someone like Audrey interacts with someone who has a high level of certainty? Certainty often comes across as being closed-minded and arrogant. But I would argue that it's not always the deeply held beliefs themselves that are received negatively as much as how they're communicated. I think Colorado is the best place to live in the United States; in fact, I'm pretty certain about it. However, I have a friend in Cincinnati who insists that Ohio is the best place to live. Both of us are pretty certain of and secure in our positions, yet this disagreement doesn't hold the same weight as religious issues often do. Why is that? Perhaps it's because religious issues are often communicated in a more zealous tone with implied eternal consequences for disagreeing. What if I started to imply that anyone who lives outside Colorado is foolish? Coloradans are happier, in better physical condition, and more enlightened. It's really pretty obvious. If you don't live in Colorado, you might be turned off by my smugness. Why would anyone want to live in a place that makes you smug? Perhaps it's not fair to compare hometown pride with religious belief, but I bet the comparison is more similar for outsiders than we might think.

Sometimes our tone of certainty reflects our actual level of certainty, but often (perhaps even more often) our tone of certainty actually reflects the level of certainty we would *like* to have. If I'm being completely honest, one of the reasons I'm so certain that Colorado is the best place to live is because I don't always believe it. At times I've second-guessed our decision to move to Colorado. When I do, I start to lean more heavily on this certainty. As it turns out, my certainty is actually an uncertainty in disguise. I don't admit uncertainty because I'm scared. What if it's true? Maybe if I keep focusing on the certainty, the uncertainty will go away. I've found that a better option for me is to confront those uncertainties and vocalize them. When I confront uncertainties and discuss them openly, they do not overcome me or change my beliefs. Rather, I find peace in what I do know and a comfort (faith) in what I don't.

I suspect that confronting our uncertainties is not only helpful to our psyche but also helpful in our interactions with outsiders. Outsiders aren't used to Christians talking about their uncertainties. As you admit yours, don't be surprised when your outsider friends follow suit and join you in a conversation.

12

SIX LESSONS LEARNED

The Things That Moved Us Most

The master praised the crooked manager! And why? Because he knew how to look after himself. Streetwise people are smarter in this regard than law-abiding citizens. They are on constant alert, looking for angles, surviving by their wits. I want you to be smart in the same way—but for what is right.

Luke 16:8–9

Have you ever taken a walk around a neighborhood you normally drive through? You notice all sorts of things you never see when you go whizzing by in the comfort of your air-conditioned car with the music blaring. Sounds, smells, human emotions, and relational drama unfold right before you when you get down on the street.

In this book the three of us decided to park our religious car and get out onto the street to experience the sights, sounds, and feelings of outsiders. We wanted to see things from their point of view. We wanted to hear what outsiders are saying, thinking, and feeling about Christianity in America on the street.

Here's what we learned about them and about ourselves.

Craig

Dialogue Is Easier Than I Thought

I hesitate to talk about my faith. With outsiders, I'm afraid to be associated with the Christian label. With insiders, I'm afraid I'll be judged for the controversial aspects of my faith. I think back to a conversation I had last spring with a tableful of conservative Minnesotans. I was at an evangelism conference, and it was my turn to share my experiences with Christianity with the group. For some reason I decided to take a risk and let them see the uncensored me. Much to my surprise, my honesty was reciprocated with curiosity and genuine interest. Under normal conditions I'd first test the waters to see if I thought they could handle it, but this conversation had me wondering if I'd been a little too guarded when talking about topics of faith in the past. Over the course of writing *The Outsider Interviews*, I've tried to be a little more open with people I disagree with, both insiders and outsiders. I've tried to participate in dialogue. And I've found that dialogue is a lot easier than I thought it would be.

In Kansas City, Klarisa and I talked openly about abortion. In Phoenix and Denver, I was able to talk with Alyssa and Andrew despite our differences. And in Seattle, I shared colorful dialogue with Audrey and Charlie. I was able to have respectful and insightful conversations about faith with all of them. Throughout this project I've caught myself in conversations about faith with the most random people in the most random places. Something has changed. I feel like a switch has been flipped and I'm now comfortable talking about faith. My Sunday school teachers would be so proud that my light is no longer under a bushel. Well, they *might* be proud—my version of "letting my light shine" looks more like an untamed bonfire than a cute flannel board candle. I catch myself being remarkably candid about my Christian upbringing, my doubts in faith, and how I now try to help Christians process why they believe what they believe through my website RecycleYourFaith.com.

I was taught that letting your light shine would be followed by persecution (which meant you were doing a good job). My version of shining doesn't get the same results. People respond by sharing their own experiences with religion and church, and a conversation is started. I used to worry about

139

how people would react to my faith, but now I feel like there's nothing to worry about. I used to try to sell a product called Christianity, but now I just share a little bit of who I am and what I'm excited about; enthusiasm helps.

I'll admit that I've been somewhat intentional in making some shifts in how I interact with people. I've had to deprogram some things I was taught and learn some new behaviors. With some hesitancy, I'm going to tell you about some of the changes I've made, but you'll have to promise not to think of these things programmatically! Basically it all boils down to me just being myself. Here's what that looks like:

1. I'm trying not to take things so personally when someone disagrees with me. Sometimes people judge me and think less of me based on my beliefs, but more often they just disagree with me.
2. I'm trying to give others permission to believe differently from the way I do. This is a mindset, not something I verbalize. I've been reminding myself as I get into difficult conversations that it's okay for someone to think differently from the way I do.
3. I'm trying to speak less in absolutes and more from personal experience. Instead of saying, "Churches are not very relevant," I might say, "In my experience I've found that churches are not very relevant."
4. As others get defensive and debate me, I try to remember that I once was and still can be a debater. Debating is a natural response to difference, and I shouldn't judge others for it. Then I try to respond with dialogue.
5. I'm trying to not jump to conclusions before really getting to know what someone thinks. It's too easy for me

to put a label on someone after a few sentences. People are more than labels.

6. I'm trying to ask lots of questions. When I start to get defensive, I try to shift that defensiveness to curiosity.

I am by no means a dialogue expert, but writing this book has taught me that despite incredible differences, dialogue is truly possible—and worth the effort.

Todd

Evangelism Boldness Never Goes Out of Style, but Styles Change

Over the years I've worn several styles of pants—or *trousers*, as our British friends say. I'm not sure any of my pants ever reached the level of *trousers*, but here is how the history of Todd Hunter's pants has unfolded. Junior high school: nothing but Levi's 501s. High school in the early 1970s: I am ashamed to say I wore the occasional big-cuffed, wide bell-bottoms! Young adult life was marked by Dockers. In

141

my later professional life I was dressed in middle-of-the-road business slacks. Presently I have an affinity for the comfort of Tommy Bahama loose-hanging silk—when I can afford it!

For the sake of my analogy, *boldness* is like pants: always on, in view at all times, permanently in play. Methods, styles, and approaches to evangelism vary with the requirements of various times and occasions. They should easily move from cotton to microfiber to silk.

But alas, this is easier said than done. We love evangelism so much that suggesting changes is unnerving and unpleasant. Saying we might change our fundamental approach to evangelism is like proposing we not have Thanksgiving dinner.

But like it or not, we are at just such a crossroads. The two or three generations reading this book need to make big changes to interact well with the outsiders we are meeting. The older parents among us need to learn the boldness of listening. Yes—it is bold to speak up, but it is even bolder to shut up and listen, to make yourself vulnerable to the assertions and questions of young outsiders.

The young Christians reading this book need the boldness to speak up. Go back and watch Andrew on the Denver Outsiders Interview. He modeled something very close to what I'm trying to express. He clearly loves Jesus and has devoted his life to helping others encounter Jesus, but he shared that confidence with a boldness wrapped in humility and authenticity, and most of all *he listened*.

There is nothing wrong with being confident in your relationship with Jesus, but as Andrew graciously modeled, that does not mean you have to become unkind, arrogant, or a know-it-all. You are a Christian today because someone had courage on your behalf. Someone took the risk to start a conversation. Someone ignored the butterflies in their stomach to try to say just the right thing to you.

The boldness to listen, to participate in a conversation about faith—this is evangelism for our time.

Jim

Collaborate or Die

I first saw this slogan about ten years ago. A man dressed in a business suit stood on the steps of a courthouse looking all protest-y, holding a placard-type sign with the words "Collaborate or Die!" high above his head. I thought it was a cool marketing campaign, but I failed to realize how sociologically prescient it was.

From Kansas City to Seattle we heard insiders and outsiders calling for unity. Where we expected deep difference, we discovered radical acceptance. What many of us call compromise, they call connection. Brand loyalty is on the bubble, but community loyalty has never been stronger.

The version of Christianity both Boomers and Millennials (aka the "Kinnaman cohort") inherited was largely developed and nurtured by type A personalities like Billy Graham, Bill Bright, Bill Hybels, and Rick Warren. It was forged in the consumer culture of Christian America, which is reflected in the way church is done every weekend in over 335,000 locations. Many of the young insiders we met were raised in these churches.

While this culture shift has been brewing for several hundred years, the change has become increasingly visible over the past twenty. While Boomers have been on the main stage playing out their final act of influence, the Millennials have been backstage playing video games, waiting for them to exit. But like Columbus accidentally bumping into the Americas while looking for India, on our way to another conclusion the three of us ran into a wonderful surprise.

In these Outsider Interviews we discovered that Millennials are neither as independent nor as cynical as their Gen X cousins. They actually want input and guidance. Here's a street-view example of what I mean by this.

Audrey, one of our Seattle outsiders, shared a letter with me that she wrote to her boss outlining five things she'd like him to know about how she sees things (if he was interested). The letter was never sent (for reasons that will become apparent), but Audrey's insights and appeals provide *an unvarnished view* of what it will take if we're serious about constructing a bridge between generations:

1. Give me things you expect me to research. Don't assume that any research I might do that exposes different viewpoints from yours (the boss's) is because I'm being insubordinate.

2. Give me feedback all the time. I'm used to instant communication, and if you want me to stay connected to you and this organization, I have to feel like we're in conversation (and hopefully dialogue).

3. Ask me what skills I want to build for my next position—and help me build them. All of us pretending that I'm going to stay in any job longer than a few years (or maybe even a field for longer than a few years) is silly, and being able to be honest about what I want and why I'm in a given job will help us be more open and honest in general.

4. Ask me about the changes I would make if I was in charge of everything, sincerely listen to my answer, and at least consider implementing a few of the ideas. (Bonus points if you let me help implement them, and double word score if you make it public that it was my idea.) The more opportunities you give me to get out, learn something new, and bring that knowledge back, the longer you'll keep me at this company.

5. Don't let *anyone* make negative comments regarding my age (or lack of experience, etc.). If it wouldn't be kosher to say, "You're decrepit!" it's not kosher to say, "You're a baby!" Don't make me defend myself on this; be the boss (man up!) and take it upon yourself to confront any kind of discrimination immediately. This is maybe the most common form of harassment I've experienced, and I've never had a boss stick up for me.

Do you feel the frustration and pain in Audrey's voice when she says, "I've *never* had a boss stick up for me"? People who are competing for the same position have no interest in protecting the person they're vying against, but coaches do. If we want to build a bridge to Millennials, then Boomers like me will have to begin thinking more like coaches and less like players.

Because Audrey is a Millennial, she *assumes* shared power. She knows she will get it sooner or later. She would just prefer to have it handed over graciously rather than wresting it from the death grip of her last Boomer boss.

Electricity results when you connect positive and negative poles. Look around you and name one man-made object you see that has not been touched by electricity. Here's my point: *innovation lies at the intersection of difference.*

From my point of view, Boomers have an activist streak and Millennials have an optimistic one. When these differences intersect, a unique force field is created that can facilitate the building of a bridge not only for themselves but for all the outsiders who are trying to find their way into the kingdom. When intergenerational activists and optimists collaborate, innovative practices and unpredictable acts of love emerge.

Craig

Dialogue Is Harder Than I Thought

How can dialogue be both easier *and* harder than I thought? I guess it all depends on *who* you're talking to. I could continue to process why some people are harder to dialogue with than others, but the fact will still remain: we will always have people in our lives who seem utterly impossible to talk to. In lieu of solving that problem, I thought I'd offer a few things I'm looking for from people I find difficult to talk with:

1. Treat me with some dignity. You may think I am dead wrong, but the more you tell me I'm wrong, the less I'm going to listen to you.
2. Don't try to prove me wrong. If you'd like to share how you've come to believe a certain way, that's great, but I'm going to start tuning you out the second you start referencing absolutes I can't argue with (yes, that means Scripture).
3. When you do talk about Scripture, please keep in mind that I may approach Scripture differently from the way you do. Don't use Scripture as a weapon.
4. Pay attention when I'm talking, and don't cut me off.
5. Try asking some questions. Genuine interest goes a long way with me.
6. Don't label me or call me names. Don't call me a baby killer when I tell you about loving someone who chose to have an abortion. Don't call me a humanist when I tell you about how I respect other religions.
7. When I ask you a question, be honest with me. Tell me how you really feel, not what you think I need to hear.
8. Let me know you're invested long-term in our relationship. I view my faith as a journey, so I want to know you don't view me as a short-term project.

While there may not be quick and easy step-by-step solutions for having open conversations, I do think (in most cases) it's worth the effort.

Todd

Everything I Learned about Dialogue Since I Knew It All

In the "Phoenix Outsiders" chapter, Jim wrote about my not-so-brilliant conversation with Erin and Abdo. He was nice about it onstage—always a professional—and even kind in his retelling. But I know him well enough to know that in the moment he was probably really thinking, *I cannot believe my friend Todd is being so stupid—and on camera!*

But come on . . . someone defend me here. Who would ever think *lost* is such a complicated word? I *lost* my car keys. What's hard to understand about that? Well, nothing, but as I talk about in chapter 4, "Things Change," everything is understood in a certain context.

148

Working with Craig and Jim and my new outsider friends, I learned that even though I have taught on evangelistic listening and dialogue all over the country and in several seminaries, there was more I needed to know *since I knew it all*. I needed a deeper experiential knowledge to augment my intellectual knowledge.

With that in mind, here are a few more details about dialogue that I picked up on while writing this book:

1. My presuppositions always need to be checked. They are not evil or to be ignored. There is no way to do life without hypotheses or working assumptions. Just don't marry them. Get hitched to your conversation partner, checking your presumptions as you go.
2. I'm not as neutral or as good as I think I am—at least I cannot assume I will be experienced that way by outsiders. Self-awareness is the door to dialogue.
3. Outsiders—"they"—are not as closed-minded or God-forsaken as I may think. We've heard it so many times that I fear it no longer penetrates our consciousness or that we reject it as New Age, but it is true: the vast majority of outsiders genuinely desire a spiritual life. They would love to talk about it if they could find some good dialogue partners.
4. We need a little less *us* and *them* and a little more *we*. This would get us a long way down the street called dialogue. When we come across as fully knowledgeable or having fully arrived at conclusions, we are not very good conversation partners. Craig and our outsider friends seem to know this really well. They are natives. I am migrating there.

5. One final, crucial thought: listening and the capacity for dialogue are first a quality of being, not an evangelistic tactic. Working the classic Christian disciplines in pursuit of spiritual transformation, we must become the kind of persons for whom open-hearted, honest, noncoercive dialogue is natural, normal, and routine.

You know what I think? If Jesus were speaking in public today, maybe he would amend his words to include that it is *out of the abundance of the heart the ear does listen and the mouth does dialogue.*

 Jim

The Urge to Serve

Hands down, the single most dominant theme to emerge from our interviewees regardless of location or religion was this: "We want to serve others." We heard it from Rio who is gay, Sam the non-Christian Christian, Alex the Christian pre-med student, Matt the Young Life worker, and Charlie the atheist. Outsiders, insiders—they've all got *the urge to serve.*

I was taught to explain this impulse among outsiders as their effort to "earn heaven." My intention is not to minimize the reality of heaven or the fact that some people may believe they will get there through good works, but at least among the people we talked with, the topic of heaven (or for that matter, fear of hell) almost never came up, including from the Christians.

I don't know what happened to talking about the rapture or end times (some of the key selling points I was taught to utilize in the early days of my Christian experience), but it appears from our work on the street that something has changed. The focus seems to have shifted from *getting humans to heaven* to *getting heaven to humans.* I was trained to believe that getting people to heaven was job number one. Now the focus among young insiders seems to have shifted to helping make the world a better place.

I realize that this might make older insiders nervous, but here's the good news: even though young Christians want to make the world a better, safer, cleaner, and more just place, this doesn't mean they've abandoned the hope of heaven or stopped wanting their outsider friends to join them there. They've simply found common ground on which to stand with their outsider friends and a way to express their faith that is more practical.

My hunch is that many young insiders who were raised in consumerist Christianity have grown weary hearing about how to make *their* lives more abundant. If current research on Christian marriage is to be believed, at least half of these insiders have watched their parents get divorced or devote the best of their lives to accumulating things on earth while talking about how great it will be to go to heaven someday. This mixed message has caused young insiders to double-check their spiritual goals. Combine that with the growing global awareness, facilitated in no small part by the internet (Google, Facebook, and Twitter to be specific), that millions of people are *already suffering a hellish existence* and you begin to understand why insiders are requiring a more practical expression of the gospel. Someone put it this way: young insiders want a little less Billy G. and a little more MLK.

The good news is that outsiders want the same thing. We can't be sure why, but for whatever reason more and more outsiders are devoting themselves to serving others as well. Frankly, from an evangelistic perspective, it's an opportunity the church can't afford to ignore. Outsiders like Audrey in Seattle put it plainly: "Don't invite me to church—invite me to serve." Outsiders are asking us to provide them with opportunities to make their world a better place, to advocate for the poor and powerless. In many ways they are inviting us to become better followers of Jesus.

Instead of *reaching out* to them, we join them to work for the common good. Saint Patrick did the same when he broke tradition and intentionally built his monasteries next to the village instead of far away.[1] We do our ministry work *with* outsiders—we invite them to serve with us, and we join their efforts to serve others. I think this is why Jesus said to his disciples, "I want you to be smart in the same way—but for what is right" (Luke 16:9).

My translation: follow the lead of outsiders, because when it comes to being streetwise, they're smarter than you are.

Copy them, emulate them, build relationships with them. You never know—when it's all said and done, they might be the ones waiting for you in heaven.

Coming In for a Landing

Here's a short history of Christianity attributed to Priscilla Shirer. For me, it captures the dilemma and dream for Christianity:

> In the first century in Palestine, Christianity was a community of believers.
> Then it moved to Greece and became a philosophy.
> Then it moved to Rome and became an institution.
> Then it moved to Europe and became a culture.
> Then it moved to America and became a business.[2]

There are two kinds of explorers: those who return saying "You should've been there" and those who return *with a map*. We hope this book serves as a map that

> invites you to travel to new places in your spiritual life;
> inspires you to start new relationships with outsiders, insiders, and everyone in between; and
> expands your notion about the true size of God's heart.

WHERE ARE THEY NOW?

An Update from Some of Our Outsiders

Books are like time capsules; they are a place where content gets frozen in time while everything else continues on. *The Outsider Interviews* gave readers a glimpse into the lives of sixteen young adults, but their lives have continued to move on. We tracked down as many of our outsiders as we could nearly three years after the interviews and asked them to send us an update. Here's what they wrote.

Sarah
(Kansas City)

Since the taping of the Outsider Interviews, I have moved to Chicago, Illinois, met and married my husband, and had a beautiful baby girl, and we have another baby on the way! I still work as a flight attendant for Southwest Airlines. My views toward Christianity have not changed in the sense that I was a Christian when we filmed and I am still a Christian. However, I was a very new Christian then, and I feel like I have grown a lot in my Christianity.

I feel like from reading the Bible, spending time in prayer, attending church regularly, and marrying a godly man, I now have a much better understanding of what it really means to be a Christian. Even some of the views that I expressed in the video have changed, but I think it's important for people who are seeking Christianity to understand that this is pretty normal. We're always changing, growing, and evolving, and we will never have all the answers. And by listening to God and spending time with him, we get to know him much better!

I'm not sure if the views of Christianity in America have changed since the interviews. I think it's becoming harder for us as Christians to express our beliefs on the tough issues, because society has put this stigma on anyone who isn't tolerant or accepting of certain lifestyles and choices that don't match up with what the Bible says. So I think Christians have been labeled as narrow-minded, intolerant people. I think it's becoming more important than ever to really listen to outsiders, but where I really struggle is in having the courage to express my own beliefs in a respectful, tactful way. I think the best way to connect with someone with different beliefs is to listen to them, respect what they are saying, and be honest about my own beliefs, and the most important thing is to stay in their life and continue to show them that I love them no matter what. I don't believe someone is going to listen to what I have to say unless they respect me, and they're not going to respect me until they've had time to get to know me.

Brian
(Phoenix)

I continue to live in Arizona, working on my PhD in chemistry. My views toward Jesus have not changed too much, though I have come to understand Christianity in the United States better. I have become increasingly aware of a church culture defined by knowing about God but not necessarily knowing him—reading the book without ever meeting the author, so to speak. This has limited the church to simply ministering the knowledge of right and wrong.

I have perceived that the church is disempowered and is lashing out destructively, powerless to change itself and the world around it, preoccupied with what is right and wrong. I have not seen a change in the perception of Christianity in the US. Politics and Christianity are still too closely interwoven. I think a lot of damage is done in trying to make America Christian and in the complaining that follows when the church realizes that America is not Christian anymore. America never was meant to be Christian; the church was.

We should ask ourselves, "Do I want to preserve corpses or bring corpses to life?" Legislating morality can only preserve the appearance of a moral standard; it can't transform an individual to love that standard. The Old Testament is evidence that you can't change people by legislating morality. The power to change is in having our desires changed to love what is good by the Spirit of God, not by knowing what is wrong.

We should focus on getting to know God, experiencing him, and sharing life with practical love. The US is a democracy, so the majority wins. We would do well to care about the hearts of the people voting instead of focusing on what the majority's vote represents.

Lastly, ministering is not about distinguishing right from wrong, it is about causing the growth of the new nature. In a plant, pruning helps it to grow better, but it does not cause it to grow; sunshine, water, and nutrients do this. If we focus expressly on chastising the desires of the old nature, we fail to cause the new nature to grow. Let's learn what the sunlight, water, and nutrients are for our new natures and then learn how to minister these things to one another.

Klarissa
(Kansas City)

I still live in Kansas City and now work at the Blue Moose Bar and Grill, where I am a server. Since the interview, I've become a follower of Jesus, and in 2009 I was baptized at Christ Church, where I am now a member. I am planning to get confirmed. I am also part of the leadership team for Alpha at Christ Church.

I still feel that Christianity is viewed the same as it was then. I think some churches are trying harder to reach outsiders and do things to help the community; however, I think there are still many churches that put a bad image on Christianity. I still think listening is a huge part of building relationships. I think building a relationship is critical in connecting with people, and when doing this, you let them know that you aren't trying to change their views. I think that it shows you just want to be a friend.

Recently I met a lady in Alpha, and she wanted to start doing a Bible study with someone. I volunteered to be that person. We have started meeting every Friday, and I let her choose what we are doing. There are days when we don't even talk about the Bible; she just shares her concerns about being a Christian and asks questions about Christianity. There are also days when we do read the Bible.

She recently shared in an Alpha interview how nice it is for her just to come and talk to me and build a relationship with me. This is how I started with Kirk. When I first met him, it was just talking about what was going on in my life and questions about what Christianity is all about. Now I am baptized and a member of a church. I think if more Christians would do this with people, there would slowly be fewer outsiders in the world.

Chandra
(Seattle)

I am currently living in Seattle after spending two years living in LA, where I began a career in the entertainment industry as an actress, writer, and producer. As of fall 2011, I am producing a Web series with one of my longtime friends, and in the summer of 2011 I started my own production company, Girl Power Productions, Inc.

I've spent most of the three years since the Outsider Interviews away from the church. I found myself in a place where I felt the same exact things toward the church that most outsiders feel. The phrase "insider outsiders" from the book really spoke to where I feel I've been within the church most of my life. I've come to realize that I actually like to be more "in the church, not of the church," and my personal journey in faith has not led me away from God but has led me away from most of the American Christian culture.

My best friends continue to be people who are agnostic or atheists/theists. I am told all the time that I am the most friendly, open, and honest Christian they have ever met. I think it's because I don't just listen, I also admit what I don't know or don't understand about my faith. Taking this approach allows me to connect on a more human and emotional level.

I don't defend my faith; I don't feel Jesus needs defending, therefore my conversations with people of different beliefs stem from wanting to get to know them as a person and understand what makes them believe what they do, not "convert" them. This has allowed me to have conversations about faith, love, heaven, and hell without getting into fights or being defensive, which in turn strengthens my own faith and has helped heal some wounds my friends have experienced at the hands of well-meaning Christians.

I currently attend church at Rain City Church in Bellevue, Washington. We meet in a movie theater and provide a safe place for people to probe their faith without feeling like they are the ones getting probed.

Andrew
(Denver)

When we did the Outsider Interviews, I had just recently moved back to Denver after two years out in Kansas City. I was starting a full-time job with Child Evangelism Fellowship (CEF) and beginning part-time classes at Metropolitan State College of Denver. I was living with my parents at the time. I am still working full time with CEF and studying part time at Metro, but I have since moved into my own condo, which I am renting with a buddy of mine.

I don't think that my views of Christianity have changed substantially since the interview, but my experience has. When I was in Kansas City, I was part of a strong young-adult community at my church there. When I came back to Denver, I had the privilege to be a part of another strong young-adult community at my church here (Bear Valley Church in Lakewood). However, between summer 2009 and summer 2010, most of my close friends in that community ended up moving out of state for various reasons. I found myself without a strong sense of community for the first time in several years.

Instead of getting connected with new people, I drifted away from the local church. For about a year (from summer 2010 to summer 2011), I had almost zero involvement with the local church. I wasn't attending Sunday worship services, and I wasn't making any meaningful attempt to connect to God on my own either. This was a hard time for me. This summer, I have started visiting Red Rocks Church in Golden. I even got plugged into a small-group Bible study there a couple weeks ago. It has been powerful and refreshing.

I would still not describe myself as "close to God," but I want him again, and that is a significant development. My year away from church—although hard and merely an external manifestation of what was going on internally in my heart—taught me something. It taught me a little bit more of what the world must be like for non-Christians. I hear Christians worrying about how to show that the church is relevant and that Christ is relevant, but non-Christian people don't think about these things. It does not even occur to them to visit a church on a Sunday morning. It does not occur to them to read the Bible. They know about Christ, but they don't think about him. They are trying to pay their bills, make ends meet, find good relationships, do a good job raising their kids, and just generally find a way to get by. Maybe if we spent less time worrying about whether they know about church or think about Christ—which, despite the best of intentions, are usually fairly self-absorbed worries for us—and spent more time *being Christ* to and among people, all these other things that we worry about would be given to us as well.

Dan
(Kansas City)

The biggest change in my life since the interview would be the change in my career. In April of 2011 I was let go from my sales position, which, while painful, has really given me time to think about my life. I took the summer off and worked on a music festival tour, and I am preparing to open a restaurant with a great friend and business partner. I am still in Kansas City and loving it.

My views on religion really haven't changed since I took part in the interview. I would say that, if anything, I have chosen to spend less time thinking about it and more time getting my life in the right direction and focusing on the state of our country. I think Christianity is having a really hard time right now in America due in large part to the fact that the majority of churchgoing people just aren't going as much or at all. Many Christians I know are more focused on their jobs and family, and religion has taken a backseat to economic worry to some degree.

My advice for Christians today would be to keep religious views out of the conversation until you have gauged that person's comfort level on the subject. I walked away from a conversation the other week due to the fact that when the person found out I was atheist, he went right into talking about how great God is. I have found that, like with any other topic, if there is a mutual want and desire to talk, the conversation will just happen.

Matt
(Seattle)

Since my experience with the Outsider Interviews, much has changed in my life. I left my job working with youth so I could start pursuing a masters of divinity at Seattle Pacific Seminary (which is part of Seattle Pacific University), and I am in my second of three years of the program. I also married an amazing woman from my seminary in December 2011. I'm backpacking and alpine climbing whenever I get the chance, and I'm interning at my church. I also started a wedding photography business, which funds these other activities and allows me to stay creative.

165

My views toward Christianity have changed since the interviews in significant and complicated ways. I am still actively growing and developing my faith, and I continue my life mission to "Love God and love people." My experience in seminary so far has created more questions than it has answered, and it has changed how I view God and read the Bible. I am developing the tools I need to better understand what my role is as a Christian and as a follower of Christ.

I'm optimistic about the future of Christianity, as people are beginning to understand that God and how people choose (or choose not) to follow God are not as black-and-white as we perhaps once thought. Christians act out their faith in many different ways, and my hope is that we can "agree to disagree" and unite as God's people before branding Christianity in a certain way. But this requires humility—lots of it. One of the most practical ways for Christians to engage those who don't share our beliefs is to start the conversation as equals. Let's not approach each other as "outsiders" but as fellow humans who are trying to understand each other and make sense of it all.

Alexandra
(Denver)

This past May, I made what I deem as the biggest move of my life to Washington, DC! I moved to attend graduate school at George Washington University. I have begun a three-year dual masters program and am studying public health and studying to become a physician's assistant. So I went from being a happy-go-lucky dermatology medical assistant and spinning instructor living and playing in Boulder, Colorado, to an overwhelmed student existing in the fast-paced hustle and bustle of our nation's capital, where it is impossible to escape politics and activism (which I secretly love but am too proud to admit it). So, yes, there have been some massive changes in my life. But like my mentor Marty Nunez says, "Change is the only consistent thing in life, so you'd better get used to it."

My views toward Christianity haven't really changed. I am still very much a liberal-minded person who loves having a deep and personal relationship with a faithful, trustworthy, grace-giving, and mysterious Lord. Furthermore, I continue to love learning from Jesus and his unconditional and passionate love for the unloved, underserved, and desperate. I *love* thinking about his humanitarian spirit and his relentless pursuit to love all people regardless of their socioeconomic status, gender, sexuality, political affiliation, race or ethnicity, and religion. More so, I love applying his unconditional love to both my academic and professional careers of caring for individuals and populations through medicine, community involvement, and most importantly, compassion. I love Jesus and I hope that, more than ever, we as Christians can stop having politically affiliated faiths and instead thoughtfully and intentionally promote and exemplify what Jesus came and died for: *hope*, *faith*, and *love*.

Tony
(Kansas City)

I still live in Kansas City and continue to work as a special education teacher for Kansas City, Kansas Public Schools. I am now married and a father of a five-month-old daughter. I continue to go to church and am actually beginning to get more involved than I have been in the past several years. I have for the most part just been an attendee and not been very serious about my relationship with Christ for four or five years, so it is a welcome change that I am desiring to get more involved with church and rekindle my passion for Christ.

I still believe the church does a bad job of showing Christ's love in the midst of taking hard moral/spiritual stances on subjects such as homosexuality and abortion, which are so divisive. I believe, increasingly, probably even more so since the Outsider Interviews, that the church is in a position where it is intellectually persecuted. Loud opponents like Bill Maher are very well-spoken and form seemingly sound arguments on why they are skeptical and why Christians (and religious/ spiritual people in general) are closed-minded, superstitious fools. I think that nonbelievers of any background probably believe this about Christians. I also think that groups on the radical fringes of Christianity, such as Kansas's very own

Westboro Baptist Church, continue to set back the church's (body of Christ's) message and progress, making us look like some backwoods group that stepped out of the Dark Ages, irrelevant and mindless of the complex situations that face American and global society.

Mainstream America is embracing women's issues/power, homosexuality, and people with special needs at an increasingly progressive rate (or at least the entertainment industry would have us believe so), and the church has failed to address these in a comprehensive, Christlike way. In short, Christianity is being marginalized as something that only conservative, closed-minded, judgmental people adhere to and not something to be taken seriously. American Christians are probably not in danger of physical persecution, but intellectually we are battered and bruised.

As for advice for Christians, I think that you should treat every person as a person, not as some trait they have. I have learned that from my experience as a special education teacher. My students are not their disability. They are people *with* a disability. I think that is how the church needs to address our most explosive societal issue: homosexuality. Every conversation with a homosexual person should not be to convert them or get them to give up homosexuality. They are more than "homosexuality"; they have lives, problems, and accomplishments that likely do not center around their sexual preferences. Treating people like people instead of focusing on the sin in their lives is probably a better approach to making lasting relationships. If there is an example to take away from the Bible, it is that Jesus most often met people where they were at. He met their needs, showed them grace and kindness, and let them come to their own realizations about their sins.

A READING GUIDE FOR GROUPS AND INDIVIDUALS

The purpose of this guide is to help you continue processing the content of this book either in a group setting or on your own. We hope it helps you grapple with the implications of *The Outsider Interviews* and incorporate what you have learned into your daily life. For each chapter we offer a few introductory statements and then questions and comments to consider. Enjoy.

Chapter 1: The Backstory

Welcome to our story. Be sure to "watch this book." Our journey into the lives of outsiders impacted us on a deep level. We think it will do the same for you when you watch the free videos online.

Questions to Consider

1. Craig suggests that various groups inside and outside Christianity have become entrenched in their views. Have you noticed this as well? How?
2. Craig suggests that trying to better understand another's perspective is a useful skill in navigating difference. What has helped you better understand another's perspective in the past? Is there room for improvement?
3. When it comes to adopting new ideas or practices, some of us are bold explorers and more of us are reluctant travelers. Which category do you fit in? How have you struggled with accepting people who are different from you?
4. Who in your life have you found difficult to interact with? Do you think there is any hope for the interactions improving?
5. *The Outsider Interviews* tells stories reflecting the statistics presented in *unChristian*. How do you respond differently to stories than statistics?

Chapter 2: Kansas City Outsiders

Being critiqued is tough. It's hard to avoid reacting and defending ourselves. We don't like it when people compare our worst with their best. But every now and again it's necessary all the same.

Questions to Consider

1. If you're a Christian, having now heard the critique of some outsiders, how does their critique make you

feel? Do you agree or disagree with their perceptions? Explain.

2. Jesus was easy on outsiders and tough on insiders. How have you seen Christians follow or not follow Jesus's example?

3. The authors suggest that when it comes to understanding the current culture, some people are natives and others are immigrants. Into which category do you fit? What do you think are the implications of this?

4. In the clip "Insiders and Gay People," Tony (who is a Christian) says two things: (1) Jesus would have hung out with gay people, but (2) Jesus *would* have had an opinion about their moral choices. How does Tony's view compare with your own view of how Jesus would handle this issue?

5. Watch the clip "An Outsider's Difficult Choice." Klarisa speaks transparently about her painful decision to have an abortion and the support her Christian friend provided. Have you ever experienced a moral dilemma and sought the support of Christians? What was the response?

6. Jim talks about the powerful influence "Christian consultants" can have on outsiders. Share about a situation when an outsider invited you to be his or her Christian consultant.

7. Tell about a time someone listened to you when you really needed it and the impact it had on your life.

Chapter 3: Klarisa Gets Saved

Can people come to faith simply because they are listened to by believers? That's what Kirk wondered, and that's what happened to Klarisa.

Questions to Consider

1. Do you think Kirk and Klarisa's story addresses the questions Jim presents at the beginning of the chapter (Should I invite my friend to church, etc.)? How or how not?
2. Kirk expanded his exposure with outsiders by spending his mornings at one Starbucks location. Are you happy with the amount of exposure you have with outsiders? What does that look like, or how might it improve?
3. Kirk's Starbucks visits are both intentional and non-intentional. How do you balance actively pursuing relationships without being pushy?

Chapter 4: Things Change

Post-Christian. Postmodern. The new atheism. Welcome to *your* culture. Church steeples disappear while cell phone towers rise. Not exactly your grandparents' world, is it?

Just as Paul leveraged Roman culture to advance the gospel in the first century, Billy Graham used "every modern means" available in the twentieth century. Both men were "anchored to the rock and geared to the times." Both men navigated their culture, and even exploited it to advance the gospel, without being consumed or controlled by it.

What about us, the twenty-first-century church? Are we willing to follow Paul's challenge to the Corinthian Christians? "I kept my bearings in Christ—but I entered their world and tried *to experience things from their point of view*" (1 Cor. 9:22, emphasis added).

Questions to Consider

1. What is your perception of how Billy Graham influenced modern-day Christianity? Share *your* Billy Graham story if you have one.
2. In this chapter Todd wrote, "Outsiders believe the only thing Christians care about is being right and proving others wrong. They believe that in conversations with Christians there is an undercurrent of arrogance." Perhaps you feel this is overstated; maybe Todd is taking it too far. How would you compare your perception of Christians to the one Todd describes?
3. Todd wrote, "There is no such thing as effective evangelism that is not reflective of its cultural context." What is your favorite form of evangelism? In what cultural context was that methodology most effective?
4. Todd said risk-free ways of doing evangelism do not exist. What kinds of risks have you taken in the past to reach people with the gospel? How have you changed your evangelism methods over time? In your mind, what are the risks associated with evangelism?
5. Think of someone you would like to see follow Jesus. How have your "evangelistic attempts" gone with them? If this chapter evoked some new ideas you might apply, what are they?

Chapter 5: Phoenix Outsiders

Christians are called *believers*. Our unique set of beliefs is central to our identity. Outsiders are confused about our beliefs, while we're often blinded by them. Do your beliefs blind you?

Questions to Consider

1. Jim asked Beth to find a Muslim between the ages of sixteen and twenty-nine who would be willing to be interviewed in a church. If someone asked you to take on that task, where would you begin?

2. A Christian audience member challenged the way Jim explained the gospel to the outsiders (accept Christ and you go to heaven; reject Christ and you go to hell). Did this offend you as well? Why or why not?

3. Watch the clip "In or Out? Erin Wants to Know." Erin asks a piercing question: "How much of the Bible do you have to believe to be saved? Sixty percent? Eighty percent?" How would you answer her? What parts of the Bible confuse you?

4. Watch the clip "Navigating Opposing Worldviews." Alyssa talks about being in relationship with people who don't agree with her Christian views but are still her friends. Could you name those people in your life? How could you go about making friends with more non-Christians?

5. In the clip "I Never Met a Christian That Wasn't a Republican," Brian, a Christian from South Africa, takes issue with American Christians being one-issue voters, and Erin, an outsider, says, "I've never met a

Christian that wasn't a Republican." If Brian and Erin made these observations directly to you, how would you respond?

Chapter 6: The Big Question

Outsiders *flocked* to Jesus, even though he told them the truth. Why do you think they wanted to be with him? Was it something in his eyes, his voice, or his body language?

Questions to Consider

1. Recall a time you were invited to have coffee with someone, thinking it was a gesture of friendship, but it turned out to be a sales pitch. How did you feel about being "baited and switched"?
2. Jim suggests that the most important question to ask outsiders is *not* "If you died right now, do you know for sure you'd go to heaven?" Have you ever participated in an evangelism program that trained you to ask something unnatural or awkward? What was that experience like for you?
3. Jim estimates that 90 percent of evangelism programs violate the Golden Rule—they fail to meet the standard of "loving others the way you want to be loved." Is this too simplistic? How would you modify his statement?
4. Talk about an outsider you *like*—someone you would enjoy spending more time with and learning about.

Chapter 7: Putting *The Outsider Interviews* to Use

One of the most effective uses of this book and video has been in the classroom. Dr. Todd Hunter has used this material many times in his training of young leaders and seminarians.

Questions to Consider

1. Todd discusses how his students and fellow professors have learned from the interviews. What have you learned so far? What have you found most interesting or surprising?

2. Todd relates a story from *Little Bee* where a Nigerian village misunderstands the context of *Top Gun*. Describe a time when you've misjudged a situation or person only to find out the true context later.

3. Todd describes a "my way or the highway" mentality that has often been adopted in evangelism. Do you find it difficult to not control others' views?

4. Todd suggests that *knowing* something doesn't exclude you from being a good conversation partner. Outsiders in our interviews have said that Christians often come across as smug or arrogant. How do you balance knowing with not being smug?

5. Todd attributes one student's response to the interviews to her being raised in a Christian bubble. Did you find the interviews surprising or unrealistic? What positives and negatives come from protecting ourselves and our children from secular culture?

6. What comes to mind when you think of the word *tolerance*? Todd writes, "Tolerance, rightly understood, is an act of love, generosity, and hospitality. Tolerance does

not demand that someone enter the conversation with us the way we wish they were. It accepts others as they are—really." Does Todd's definition of tolerance work for you?

Chapter 8: Denver Outsiders

Birds of a feather flock together, and so do Christians. *Difference* makes us uncomfortable, afraid, and sometimes angry. Separating ourselves from difference has even become a sign of maturity for Christians. But what if one of *your* friends "goes different" on you? What then? It's happening all around us. It may have already happened to you.

Questions to Consider

1. If you watched the Denver interview with a group, share with each other the feelings it prompted or provoked in you. Try not to correct, fix, or analyze each other's feelings. Just listen. If you're not in a group, simply note what emotions came up for you when you watched this interview.

2. In the clip "Remaining Open," Andrew talks about holding some things with a closed hand and others with an open hand. What issues do you hold with a closed hand, and what issues do you hold with an open hand?

3. What do you find most interesting or surprising about the video clip "Backstage in Denver"?

4. Watch the clip "The Christian Label" in the Denver section of the website. What label or description do

you use to explain your faith or beliefs? How do other Christians and/or outsiders respond to this?

Chapter 9: Getting Past Gay

We think this might be the most important chapter of the book. We wrote *The Outsider Interviews* in part to help parents understand their kids. Things change. Today's twenty-somethings are different from those of earlier generations. That's why Craig wrote this chapter.

Questions to Consider

1. Craig said, "I started a process I now call 'recycling my faith,' where I pressed the reset button and started over. I kept some beliefs and discarded others, but I primarily reshaped the things I'd been taught to better reflect my personal experience with God. I call this recycling because I didn't just discard the faith I grew up with; rather, I reused and redeemed parts of it so that it could be useful in my life today. I began to trust myself and Jesus a little more and what I'd been taught a little less." Does Craig's term "recycling faith" work for you? Why or why not? What beliefs have you recycled?

2. Craig said to his father, "I don't see us coming to any conclusions about that topic. I just want to explore whether it's possible for us to talk about something like homosexuality without it resulting in an anger-filled, intellectual debate." We have difficulty talking about differences. The categories that most often trigger these kinds of feelings seem to be religion, politics, and

sexuality. In what relationships have you been able to talk about these sensitive topics without the relationship falling apart? What is necessary for such an interaction to take place?

3. At one point Craig apologizes to his dad for judging him. Have you ever apologized to your parents or anyone else for judging them? How did that experience change you? How did it impact the relationship?

4. Craig's dad expresses frustration with homosexuals who "seem hyper-sure of themselves" and "want to shove their lifestyle in our faces by parading their relationships and complaining about not having equal rights." Gay people, of course, accuse Christians of the very same practices. What do you make of this dynamic? How might Christians engage it constructively?

5. Craig summarizes what he wants from his dad this way: "I just want to feel as though he accepts me even if he disagrees with me." Why do you think this is so important to Craig?

6. This chapter doesn't have a happy ending. That's because Craig and his dad remain in a process. Lack of resolution is frustrating. Are you in a relationship that is to some extent unresolved? If so, what is difficult about this? What gives you hope about your relationship?

Chapter 10: The Risky Business of Engaging Difference

What happens when there's no happy ending? We don't like it, but the fact is that when we tell the truth, it can cost us. Craig Spinks takes you behind the scenes in his family drama.

Questions to Consider

1. What were your first reactions after reading the continuation of Craig's story? Who did you find yourself relating to in the story?
2. Do you have a family member you find hard to interact with at times? How do family dynamics help or hinder your interactions with that person?
3. It seems that Craig is trying to change how he interacts with his family to more closely reflect his interaction with people outside his family. Do you think that family interactions should be thought of differently than other relationships, or should all relationships essentially play by the same rules?
4. At the end of the chapter, Craig says that his goal isn't to eliminate pain but to learn how to move through painful experiences in a more healthy way. How do you typically respond to painful experiences? How would you like to respond?

Chapter 11: Seattle Outsiders

This chapter addresses two issues: (1) outsiders' and insiders' perception that Christianity is overly involved in politics, and (2) outsiders' and insiders' desire to serve others.

Questions to Consider

1. How do you make sense of the reality that while most African American Christians vote Democratic, most white Christians vote Republican? How would (or do) you explain this well-known divide to outsiders?

2. In the clip "The Urge to Serve," Chandra (an insider) and Audrey (an outsider) say essentially the same thing: serving others is a spiritual activity. Many Christians have been taught that outsiders' only motive for serving others is to earn a ticket to heaven (aka good works). What do you sense is Audrey's motive?

3. The clarity of Audrey's plea, "Don't invite me to church—invite me to serve," is startling to us. Even though it comes from an outsider, it captures the value shift we sense taking place among young people—both insiders and outsiders. In the past, obeying Jesus was interpreted to mean personal morality; now it includes *serving others*. Why do you think this shift is taking place? Does it concern or comfort you?

4. In the clip "Bottom Line Beliefs," Matt, Sarah, and Alex discuss what they see as foundatonal in Christain faith. What do you think is foundational? Do you have any beliefs that don't align? If so, how do you reconcile those beliefs with your Christian faith?

Chapter 12: Six Lessons Learned

With the interviews in the rearview mirror, the three of us took time to reflect. What was going on in the minds of Todd, Craig, and Jim on a deeper level? What were the things that impacted us the most?

Questions to Consider

1. Craig said, "I was at an evangelism conference, and it was my turn to share my experiences with Christianity

183

with the group. For some reason I decided to take a risk and let them see the uncensored me." Have you, like Craig, shared your real feelings with some Christians, knowing you were taking a risk? If so, what happened?

2. Todd said, "It is bold to speak up, but it is even bolder to shut up and listen, to make yourself vulnerable to the assertions and questions of young outsiders." Todd flips the meaning of boldness from preaching to listening. When have you exercised the courage of listening to people say something you really didn't want to hear? Upon reflection, was it a good decision? How did it impact that relationship?

3. Jim said, "Audrey, one of our Seattle outsiders, shared a letter with me that she wrote to her boss, outlining five things she'd like him to know about how she sees things (if he was interested)." Review Audrey's list. Which points do you identify with, and which ones seem over the top? Why?

4. Craig said, "I could continue to process why some people are harder to dialogue with than others, but the fact will still remain: we will always have people in our lives who seem utterly impossible to talk to. In lieu of solving that problem, I thought I'd offer a few things I'm looking for from people I find difficult to talk with." Review Craig's list. Which of his points pushes your buttons, and why do they do so?

5. Todd said, "Listening and the capacity for dialogue are first a quality of being, not an evangelistic tactic. Working the classic Christian disciplines in pursuit of spiritual transformation, we must become the kind of persons for whom open-hearted, honest, noncoercive

dialogue is natural, normal, and routine." If, as Todd suggests, evangelism meant the spiritual practice of noncoercive dialogue, how would that change the way you share Jesus with people?

6. What opportunities do you have to stand on common ground and work for the common good with the outsiders in your life? What can you do this week to begin cultivating those opportunities?

Chapter 13: Where Are They Now?

We were able to check back with our original guests to find out how things had or hadn't changed in their lives and perspectives.

Questions to Consider

1. When you reached this chapter, which of the outsiders were you looking forward to hearing from the most? Why?
2. Whose update surprised you the most?
3. A number of the updates included shifts in thought or belief. Do you find this fluidity encouraging or discouraging? Why?

NOTES

Chapter 1 The Backstory

1. David Kinnaman and Gabe Lyons, *unChristian: What a New Generation Really Thinks about Christianity . . . and Why It Matters* (Grand Rapids: Baker, 2007).

Chapter 4 Things Change

1. Kinnaman and Lyons, *unChristian*, 15, 24, 33.

2. Ibid., 26.

3. Ibid., chaps. 2 and 3.

4. Ibid., 25.

5. Ibid., 29.

6. From everything I know from being around Billy Graham just a little bit, from everything I have read, and from those mutual acquaintances between Graham and myself, I know that Billy would not like attention being drawn to himself in any untoward way. I am quite sure he thinks of himself as just a man, a blessed and gifted servant of the gospel.

7. William Martin, *A Prophet with Honor: The Billy Graham Story* (New York: Harper, 1992), 93.

8. Ibid.

9. John Pollock, *Billy Graham: The Authorized Biography* (New York: McGraw-Hill, 1968), 56.

10. Ibid., 51, 61; Martin, *A Prophet with Honor*, 91.

11. Kinnaman and Lyons, *unChristian*, 71.

12. "Inquirer" was the name given to outsiders before "seeker" became the norm.

13. These ideas come mostly from a November 2006 *Wired* feature article by Gary Wolf titled "The Church of the Non-Believers." See http://www.wired.com/wired/archive/14.11/atheism.html.

14. "In God's Name," *The Economist*, Nov. 1, 2007, available online at http://www.economist.com/node/10015255.

15. See especially chaps. 1–3.

Chapter 6 The Big Question

1. See Dan Kimball, *They Like Jesus but Not the Church: Insights from Emerging Generations* (Grand Rapids: Zondervan, 2007), 42–43.

2. See Brian McLaren, *More Ready Than You Realize: The Power of Everyday Conversations* (Grand Rapids: Zondervan, 2002) for the best example of the power of noticing.

Chapter 7 Putting *The Outsider Interviews* to Use

1. Chris Cleave, *Little Bee* (New York: Simon and Schuster, 2008), 66; italics in original.

Chapter 9 Getting Past Gay

1. "Fifty-eight percent of young white evangelicals support some form of legal recognition of civil unions or marriage for same-sex couples" ("Survey: Young Evangelical Christians and the 2008 Election," *Religion and Ethics Newsweekly*, September 29, 2008, http://www.pbs.org/wnet/religionandethics/week1204/survey.html).

2. See Kimball, *They Like Jesus but Not the Church*, and Bruce Bickel and Stan Jantz, *I'm Fine with God . . . It's Christians I Can't Stand* (Eugene, OR: Harvest House, 2008).

Chapter 11 Seattle Outsiders

1. See Paul G. Hiebert, *Anthropological Reflections on Missiological Issues* (Grand Rapids: Baker Academic, 1994), chap. 6.

Chapter 12 Six Lessons Learned

1. George G. Hunter III, *The Celtic Way of Evangelism: How Christianity Can Reach the West . . . Again* (Nashville: Abingdon, 2000).

2. Priscilla Shirer quoted in Scott Kalevik, *Living Hope Today: A Daily Devotional* (Bloomington, IN: iUniverse, 2001), 106.

Jim Henderson is CEO of Jim Henderson Presents and author of *The Resignation of Eve*. He has also written two books on the topic of connecting with outsiders: *Evangelism without Additives* and *Jim and Casper Go to Church*. He holds a doctor of ministry degree from Bakke Graduate University. He and his wife, Barbara, live near Seattle, Washington.

Todd Hunter, bishop for The Anglican Church in North America, is the founding pastor of Holy Trinity Anglican Church in Costa Mesa, California. Author of *Christianity Beyond Belief* and *Giving Church Another Chance*, Todd is also the founding director of Churches for the Sake of Others, a West Coast church planting initiative. He is an adjunct professor of evangelism and contemporary culture at George Fox University, Fuller Seminary, Western Seminary, Vanguard University, and Wheaton College. He is past President of Alpha USA and former National Director for the Association of Vineyard Churches. Todd also founded Three Is Enough, a small group movement that makes spiritual formation doable. Todd and his wife, Debbie, have two adult children and live in Costa Mesa, California.

Craig Spinks is the owner of Quadrid Productions, a production company that specializes in capturing real-life stories that challenge, inform, and motivate. Craig also runs the website RecycleYourFaith.com, which features videos on compelling spiritual topics. Craig and his wife, Sara, live in Denver, Colorado.

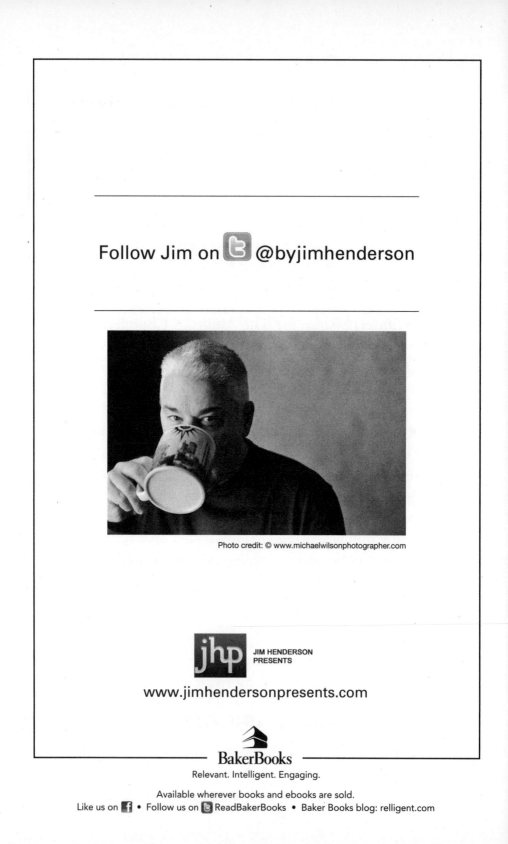

Travel to new places in your spiritual thought life.

RECYCLEYOURFAITH.COM

videos for spiritual explorers

ANGLICAN CHURCH
IN NORTH AMERICA

CHURCHES
FOR THE SAKE
OF OTHERS

Planting churches
for the sake of others

c4so.org